W0038605

Religion,

Brainwashing,

or

Spirituality

(Your Choice)

RUBY JACKSON

Religion, Brainwashing, or Spirituality
©2021, Ruby Jackson

All rights reserved. This book or any portion thereof may not be reproduced or used in any manner whatsoever without the express written permission of the publisher except for the use of brief quotations in a book review.

ISBN: 978-1-09837-163-0
ISBN eBook: 978-1-09837-164-7

DEDICATION

This book is dedicated to my dear late mother, RUBY L. JACKSON, a *strong* woman, who even during sickness in her final years, remained faithful to God, her husband, and her family. One cannot help but think she arranged for her departure directly with God as she left this earth so peacefully. To this point, some of the family have many unanswered questions and unresolved feelings; but we are not afraid to ask God certain questions concerning our loved one. We believe she was a dedicated individual to God and a very good person who devoted all her time to her husband, children, and church. To our knowledge, she never consumed alcohol or smoked. She joined the church in her pre-teen years, remaining until her last breath on earth. She always spoke positively and encouraged us to do the same. She gave her tithes faithfully and always shared both her monetary and mental wealth with others. She worshipped God each service as if it were her last. During the last few years of her life, there were times she fought through indescribable pain and circumstance due to health complications. But we reflect on the many good ones before those days as they far outweighed the bad. So, some now ask how someone so loving and dedicated to her family and God could encounter so much pain and suffering in this lifetime. But in asking for resolve, we continue to trust God. Besides, what is the point of trusting God if we only do so when things are going right? Rest on, Mother, until we meet again. ☺

Sunrise–Sunset:
July 1951–June 2015

ACKNOWLEDGEMENTS

I would like to thank, first and foremost, God for giving me the courage and wisdom to compose this book. I would also like to thank my family and friends who provided many words of encouragement and feedback on the development of the same. Without them, I may have not had the motivation or drive to continue in the pursuit of starting or completing this project. Finally, I would like to thank my mother and father, whom I love dearly, as they are the strong individuals who raised ten beautiful children and never once complained of the responsibility.

CONTENTS

FOREWORD

T HERE has long been controversy among different denominations, faiths, religious sectors, idealisms, and so forth over the path to God. Some believe there is only *one* direction to follow for a reward of eternal peace in a heavenly place above the skies and, conversely, many directions from which to choose for eternal damnation in a hell filled with fire and brimstone, with our destination, of course, being determined by our works whether good, bad, or indifferent. So, we ask ourselves: How do we know which way to take?

With so many surrounding unanswered, controversial questions said to be the detriments of our fate in the afterlife, which path does one choose? The key word is "choose." As children we may have not had a choice on which path to take. The only option was to follow the religion which our parents found suitable—well, that or hit the streets. But as we mature, hopefully, we become open to different beliefs and philosophies that expose our minds to something new, even if not taken as our truth.

The freedom of choice is not expressed enough, but the need for one to choose a path and to never deter is a dominantly expressed idea. In my short journey thus far, I believe I have experienced religion, brainwashing, and spirituality, with spirituality being the overwhelmingly satisfying form of nurture for mind, body, spirit, and *soul*. This book comes with the intent to share my personal experiences from childhood into adulthood with the three topics of discussion: religion, brainwashing, and spirituality. I hope it will help some to realize they are not alone and will provide a way to think outside of the box leading to many forms of individual freedom. Enjoy the ride.

INTRODUCTION

D o we have a choice? I am not a political person at all; but according to the First Amendment of the United States Constitution,
we have freedom of religion, which I believe is also a God-given gift.
At a certain point in consideration of age, whom one chooses to follow
should be a free exercise that comes with no ridicule or scrutiny. Of
course, in all things, I do believe moral codes of conduct should be
closely connected to one's belief system: a moral code according to a
spiritual reference and a moral code of conduct in accordance with
the laws of the land.

In the spiritual practice of moral conduct, one usually believes
in a higher essence or being. What should be of most importance to
everyone is not whom or what one chooses to believe but its satisfaction of its intended purpose. Hopefully, the chosen practice is of a
positive vibration.

Through the years, an increasing number of individuals and
groups have made it a point not only to adhere to a higher being—and
rightfully so—but also, in the same context, to attempt to discredit
others claimed by people with different perceptions. Do we have a
choice? A passage from a familiar book reads, "Choose you this day
whom ye will serve" (Josh. 24:15 KJV). Now, the leader I choose to

follow is Jesus Christ, whom I believe to be the Son of God. No, I am not testifying, just clarifying. I grew up in a Christian background from my mother's womb. In fact, my mother and father met at the church in which I was raised. There they wedded. Eventually, they had ten beautiful children. As far as I can remember, my father was a preacher at the church; so, yes, I grew up as a preacher's daughter. Growing up in that kind of background had both its rewards and challenges.

As I mentioned, as a child, I had no choice but to follow the religious path chosen by my parents. But believe it or not, that is not the main basis of my faith. It is not only because of my personal experiences inside of the church but also—and mainly—because of my personal encounters with God outside of the church that I have built a relationship external of man-made rules, regulations, restrictions, biases, witchcraft, brainwashing, and the like, which some try to connect with the interpretation of the Bible or a written doctrine. Yes, it gets deep.

Let us first delve into the religion in which I was raised and some of the learned practices. From there, we will talk about the development in age which brought enlightenment to me. Growing up, my life and those of my brothers and sisters were severely restricted due to following a very strict set of rules connected to religious beliefs and contrary to the freedom still being taught by some. Lastly, we will explore one of the lasting memories of spiritual encounters which helped me to distinguish between man-made interpretations of who God should be to me and the God I've come to know. Let's go!

PART I

GROWING UP IN A RELIGIOUS FAMILY WITH LITTLE FLEXIBILITY

CHAPTER 1:

Age and the Perception of Religion

W HAT is religion to me? Religion can be interpreted to mean many different things to different people, but my personal interpretation is a practiced belief that gives very little flexibility to change regardless of the circumstances in time. I can remember as a little girl loving to go to church. I would look forward to clapping my hands, stomping my feet, or playing the tambourine. Those movements expressed praise, gratitude, and happiness. At that time, most of my immediate family of ten (six boys and four girls) sharing the same mother and father were very much involved, some serving as different board members and singing in the church choirs.

Sunday school was also interesting, so I did not mind going or participating in some of the readings. Much was learned from those lessons. I sometimes still find myself remembering some of the valuable lessons learned, such as what a parable is in how it relates heavenly stories to earthly meanings or the great magnitude of God's love.

At that time, I viewed church as a recreational experience that I could not wait to experience on a given night. I formed many friendships and was first introduced to some of my family members that I may have not otherwise known.

During some services, I was able to see first-hand God's love and mercy when someone was delivered from drugs or alcoholism because they came to reconciliation with themselves and God, acknowledging with a determined mind they needed and wanted change. Those memorable moments helped me to establish my faith in God and the belief in his son, Jesus Christ. I too would sometimes feel the spirit of God and enjoyed every moment shared together.

I have a lot of fond memories of things that helped shape my character. I may not have seen parents who believe in God as too much of a blessing then; but, thankfully for me, the blessing is no longer in disguise.

I experienced a lot of ups and downs due to the many challenges that came with gaining an understanding of certain religious practices. More questions came as I matured in age as with age came wisdom. My perspective was starting to change regarding certain rules and regulations that seemed trivial as a child but more relevant as an adolescent and imperative as an adult.

This change in mindset was in direct correlation with the experiences I encountered as a church-going young adult and as a preacher's daughter. Growing up as a preacher's daughter had its benefits and limitations. This imbalance was due to the difficulty in managing the church and the home environments. Some of that difficulty came with my father at times not being able to distinguish operating a home from operating a church, which was due to the enforced teachings of the church. It was like attending church service 24/7, 365 days a year.

My family's personal business was sometimes in jeopardy of being exposed to the congregation. My siblings and I shared many moments of "why did you just tell our personal business over the pulpit." As far as the 24/7 button in operation at home, on many occasions scriptural text was applied to conversation that required just ordinary fatherly responses. For example, when my father thought I was on the phone too long, he referenced the scripture about temperance. Were I still living at home today, I can imagine how much I would hear it because I am now so attached to my cellular phone. To be honest, back then I did not fully understand the meaning of temperance; but I assumed it had something to do with controlling overindulgence.

Inflexibility with religious practices was sometimes a major setback to effective communication. But because this was a learned behavior enforced by the leader of the church, with whom my father happened to be very close, he had a sense of obligation to mandate 24/7. Being flexible was seen as "compromising with the devil."

I believe most can agree that not feeling free to communicate with a parent leaves a door open to communicate with someone who may not offer the best advice. Nevertheless, the advice is more readily accepted due to its genuine-like nature. Luckily, I did not have to look very far for that valuable attribute because my mother was an excellent listener and advisor, which created better balance within the home. The kids were able to find relief in Mother's advisement. In turn, some of my older brothers and sisters adopted those same skills, so we were able to also confide with each other, concerning topics that we may have been uncomfortable sharing with our mother.

Although on more than enough occasions did our father offer religious advice, he also often shared good life wisdom—which I still follow today—such as to finish school and to always save for a rainy day. I think *Rich Dad, Poor Dad's* founder, Robert Kiyosaki, would *partially* disagree as, according to him, today's savers are losers. But to further my dad's point, it is always good to have some easy-access cash in the bank. I have exercised my dad's way but am now trying to also implement some of the investment advice of the proven Robert Kiyosaki.

More inflexibility within the religion came with the requirement to attend church services at least four times a week. I support parents ensuring their children receive a religious foundation. But as children grow into adolescence, having proven responsible when left home alone, parents should look forward to them making their own decisions concerning whether to attend. If young adults are being forced to attend, it takes away from them enjoying the church experience.

I recall several instances leaving homework undone to use as an excuse to stay home on a church night. Hey, sometimes it worked, other times, not so much. Playing sick was also a tactic used to be *excused* from attendance. This pressure to attend church service lasted until I left home at the age of nineteen. My point is because it was being forced, the *love* turned into resentment. My hands stopped clapping, my feet stopped stomping, and my tambourine stopped being banged. Some may ask where the love disappeared to. I say, when we walk into a church, we should feel and see freedom to worship, to love, and to respect. Unfortunately, I started to feel and see otherwise.

To this day, I keenly remember hearing these words coming from the pulpit: "holiness or hell." Yes, to this day, I can't quite get my grasp on the concept. My understanding was it meant if we were not members of that church body or shared belief in the same, we were on our way to hell.

Back then, there was plenty of material for consumption; so, I feel the need to share one more infamous saying. Hmm, let's see . . . Okay, here's one: "Separate yourself." To the average person that would mean to mingle with like-minded people or otherwise risk being a part of a crowd that does not support our progression, which is understood. But, from the interpretation of my upbringing, it meant to completely disconnect from people, including family, who did not share the same religious beliefs as we could easily become "corrupt" with their evil doings. Intermingling was entwining with the world. A favored suggestion was for us to limit conversation with outsiders unless we were extending an invitation to church and to keep extensive communication amongst members within the church body.

It has been proven that healthy communication comes from all walks of life. The origination point should not matter as there is always someone outside of our normal circle who may be of benefit in one way or another. Connecting with people should be our way of communicating God, not just by word of mouth or by way of an invitation to church but through daily living.

For teenagers, part of the enjoyment of going to school is hanging with friends and creating new friendships. However, we were taught the people of the "world" were not our friends. I agree that good friends are very hard to find. However, that conclusion should not come from a preconceived notion but from experience. In fact, some of my best friendships were formed with people not belonging to my former church body. On the other hand, some of my greatest hurt was experienced within the church.

How is it that members of a church can help free someone from a long-time addiction then try to keep chains on them through relentless control tactics? It's simple. In the first instance, divine intervention is invited to operate; in the other, personal opinions and emotions are at the forefront of operation.

We do not have to be in the spirit of God to operate a gift. Gifts are a part of our human make-up. It is our choice how we put them to use. We may possess natural abilities which may have been inherited, such as the ability to play sports well. Then, we have those God-given gifts that are inexplicable but are manifested through our exercise of that gift while in the spirit, such as preaching or singing. It comes effortlessly and is recognized as unique because certain things can't be taught.

Then there are people who, over time, develop abilities through practice and due diligence. These come at a higher level of difficulty because they are not genetically rooted. A preacher can preach in self or under the operation of the spirit of God. The feel and delivery of the message is obviously different, which makes it easy to distinguish the two. It takes self to invite God to operate in full capacity. If not, self or another person will be in the driver's seat.

Another example is a singer who sings spirituals or messages of hope after inviting God to operate (also known as being under the anointing) and a singer who has a natural ability to sing, such as the late great Michael Jackson, who was able to sing and bring forth emotions within himself and within the audience which satisfied. Again, there is self who can do some amazing things and there is God who not only allows self to do those things but also trumps those possibilities.

Some gifts are only in operation as commanded by the spirit of God, such as the gift of prayer or healing. We have natural healers and those who can only heal when they invite the spirit of God to operate through them. Those individuals have to be in a certain mind space that is connected with the spirit of God in order to produce the desired results. If not, the results will not be as favorable as one might desire.

CHAPTER 2:

Religion and Sports

A NOTHER belief of my former religion was not to allow participation in academic team sports. This seemed to be a rule inserted just for certain families because some kids did participate. One moved on to play in a professional league. For others, involvement in gym classes was the closest one could get to participation. I have a very athletically gifted family, but our father was taught by the church leader that if playing sports interrupted the church schedule, then we could not participate. Consequently, those teachings were enforced on our lifestyle. One may ask how any sport cannot conflict with church scheduling when attending church at least four times a week. The answer is I don't believe it is reasonably possible.

Participating in academic sports has been proven to help boost confidence and increase the ability to work cohesively within a team. Most sports involve a team working together to achieve a common goal, which ultimately is to win. Nonteam sports such as tennis or golf also offer the same benefits because, at a point, we must work with and learn from others who can improve overall technique and strategy. That increases the likelihood of developing social skills.

Another factor excluding the participation in academic sports was that the females of the faith could not wear pants or shorts. Wearing shorts or pants is the uniform of choice for most sports I've come to know. At least that was the case for the ones favored by my family. Some team sports will allow skirts to be worn in place of shorts/pants, but that choice should be left to the participant. If some of this sounds familiar, it is because it is more in tune with traditional values.

Not being able to wear pants, shorts, or any skirts above our knees made for an interesting life as teenagers. I remember my peers inquiring why I didn't wear pants. I simply said, "Because it goes against my religion." Whether that was an acceptable answer to them or not was not my concern. I never fully understood why, just that it was a belief that some perceived to be supported by biblical text left open for interpretation.

Inventive ways came into play when I wanted to wear shorter skirts or slip on a pair of pants for gym. I would walk out of the house, as they say, looking holier than thou (I use that phrase loosely because I don't believe in anyone looking that way) and change into a shorter skirt, usually stolen from my older sister's closet, to suit my needs and fashion. Ultimately, I did what I wanted regardless of my outward appearance. Fortunately for me, high school was much easier because by that time skirts were more of a fad, making it easier to dress in the way I preferred, which was and still is modernly with style.

I recall in middle school, after I first started to slip into shorter skirts (above the knees) after leaving the house, getting caught by my father. Because I was an amateur, I would leave the house in a longer skirt, wearing a shorter skirt underneath; then in the backyard of my house, which happened to be nicely secluded with trees, I'd slip off the longer skirt to showcase the underneath shorter skirt for the day. That turned out to be a bad idea because whenever the weather would break, my father would sit on the indoor porch, which gave him a spectacular view of outside occurrences. One day, I was in his view as I was going into the backyard to change back into my longer skirt before my entrance into the house. As I was changing, I looked up and saw my father, making my heart seemingly drop to my feet. The look on my father's face said it all, so I prepared for the worse.

That day I received the only beating I ever received from my father. It was very painful and seemed to forever last. There is nothing like getting a butt whooping from a man.

Although I may have not participated much in academic sports, my family and I often played sports together. We qualified as gifted athletes, according to several school gym teachers who wanted us to be part of diverse academic team sports, including football, basketball, track, and volleyball. During my time in elementary school, I was the fastest female in the school, only trailing behind a few older boys for overall fastest. I was a member of my elementary school track team because I could wear skirts and the team did not conflict with church scheduling. Every now and again, I would sneak on a pair of shorts to participate. Other than that, I tried to wear looser skirts to ensure there was no interruption with stride.

I recall in the fifth grade having a track meet where everyone was depending on me to show and perform. For the meet, the school's track coach provided everyone with uniforms, which came with a pair of short tights. On the day of the meet, I went to grab the shorts but somehow my father had found where they were hidden. Needless to say, that attempt was spoiled. I arrived on the scene late; but when I finally showed, everyone was thrilled to see the fastest girl in the school.

After the many events held within the meet, we proceeded to run the last race, which was the relay race I happened to anchor. With my team in the lead, the baton was handed to me as I broke into stride. I was off to the races in my jeans skirt! Someone was quickly gaining on me, but I was still leading until . . . I fell. How humiliating! The jeans skirt I was wearing did not allow enough flexibility for my quick, long strides; it disrupted my form, ultimately causing me to fall. I wore a jeans skirt because any other skirt made of lighter material might have possibly flown up, exposing my goodies! Not to mention, in previous times, I had successfully run in the same skirt and so possibly did not foresee the challenges. Oh, wait. Let us also not forget I had planned to run in the shorts my father found instead of the jeans skirt.

Of course, I laugh at it now; but back then the only ones laughing were my teammates, who were also thoroughly disappointed. My best friend at the time, who happened to be the second fastest girl in the school and a member of the relay team, would not let up on the jokes. I guarantee to this day that if reminded of that time, she will still laugh hysterically.

After that, because I did not participate in any further track meets, I was jokingly (at least I'd like to think so) blamed for ruining professional track careers. The reason was that if I did not participate, neither would the girls on my former track squad. Hey, it wasn't my fault. ☺

Although I was a very good sprinter, which was inherited from my parents, I never really enjoyed running track. Naturally, people wanted me to run so I obliged; but one of my other sisters, who was faster, enjoyed it more so.

As a teenager, I developed a love for playing basketball. Of course, I couldn't participate on my high school team because of the shorts and church conflict issues. Even with my mother's support of my participation, had I followed through I would have had to move out of the house at the suggestion of my father.

Some of my siblings were so frustrated they started to misbehave in school and hang in the streets. Because of being so limited in living life as kids, we started to rebel. In turn, the streets were waiting to provide fabricated comfort, love, and fun. I often hear professional athletes saying how playing sports kept them out of trouble and changed their lives for the better. Could the opposite occurrence have the opposite effect?

One day on a church trip that I thoroughly enjoyed and was blessed enough to attend, most of the girls were swimming (floating for those of us who could not swim) fully clothed inside the hotel swimming pool. As you recall, the females of the religion were not allowed to wear shorts or pants, let alone bathing suits; so being in clothing while swimming was a necessity. Well, after enjoying a few minutes of swimming, due to a complaint lodged by other hotel guests, we were approached by one of the hotel attendants who asked some of us to remove ourselves from the swimming pool. The dye from our jeans skirts was disrupting the chlorine. How embarrassing!

Of course, some of us were angry because we didn't understand the logic. We were just kids having a good time. All right, we may have not been shy in voicing our opinions to the hotel attendant; but that is beside the point. ☺ The point is a little flexibility in allowing us to at least wear shorts with a bikini top or a bathing suit accompanied by a t-shirt to cover up would've been awesome. In fact, even with knowing the possible consequences, some of us proceeded to do so.

Attending sporting events was off limits as well. The explanation provided for this rule was that it was "of the world." I suppose I should be grateful I was even able to watch sports on television because my older siblings went through a phase where they were unable to do so, due to the tube being referenced as being of the "devil." In fact, in dramatic fashion, they witnessed two clergy members take a sledge-hammer to one of the televisions they were watching, destroying it. Of course, since then, the rules have evolved to allow for the watching of cable television. Woo hoo!

CHAPTER 3:

Can Religion, Career, and Family Be Balanced?

M EMBERS were to forfeit any job or offer that conflicted with church scheduling no matter the financial hardship one might have been facing. Being faithful to the church ahead of family was also important. Numerous sermons admonished people not to put family ahead of the people of the church. Putting the church members first was putting God first. Members were to keep a division between the two, with the family settling for second best of an individual or nothing at all. If a loved one did not agree with the religious followings, members were advised to cut them off. The scripture for this was, "Can two walk together except they be agreed"? (Amos 3:3 KJV).

I agree we cannot "walk" in harmony with a person if in disagreement. However, what happened if two individuals in the church did not agree with one another? According to the teachings, individuals were supposed to come together and reason. Could this not be done with someone outside of a particular church body as well? Yes, it certainly could. And it has been done more than one can count. If a certain respect level is provided on both sides where no one is negatively impacting the other or putting pressure on the other to adopt opposing beliefs, is this not agreeing to disagree on the religious level but perhaps agreeing to speak relatively on other subject matters?

I've seen in some churches that having faith and exercising faith seem identical in nature; where praying is equated to putting it in the Lord's hands. Then sitting back waiting is equated to an exercise of patience. But I believe having faith in a prayer sent to God and then exercising what is necessary to gain that request while waiting in expectance exemplifies faith and patience.

Having money to pay bills but putting a portion or all of it into the offering plate then expecting God to make another way for the lights to stay on is not the best exercise of faith, let alone of wisdom. Sometimes people may experience special circumstances in which God has told them to give their last and to trust another way will be made. Sometimes people have to make sacrifices to receive increase. However, when people, according to their own will, are consistently facing financial hardship due to giving their last to causes not in support of their own livelihood, then they need to exercise a little more wisdom. Exercising faith to increase one's income, by going back to school to gain better employment skills that lead to a better career path or entrepreneurship is a wiser choice.

I admit unique situations exist where, after we've done all we can, we have to stand and watch in exhaustion, pain, and expectance. I think those situations call for the most patience because they are out of our hands as human beings and are into God's, so trusting is our only option.

CHAPTER 4:

God Knows Your Heart or Personal Appearance?

G OD knows our hearts communicate understanding. However, during many sermons, outward appearance seemed to be the topic of discussion. If one's hair was not parted in the way liked by certain ones, one could expect it to be mentioned during the sermon.

If a clergy member did not care personally for facial hair and felt one of the members grew in a little too much, that small change in appearance was mentioned in a condescending manner before the congregation. Some of the smallest changes to haircuts or hairstyles would sometimes be mentioned. If God looks at the heart and we are followers of God, then we too should look at the heart and not focus so much on the appearance of a human being. When we go to church, we hope to look as presentable as possible. But that should not be the focus. I recall one time wearing Timberlands to church. From the pulpit, I heard, "The woman **shall not wear** that which **pertaineth** unto a **man**," (Deut. 22:5 KJV), followed by a description of the Timberlands some of the other girls and I were wearing. Of course, the word I said then and say to that now is precisely the same, "PLEASE!" Where was God in the building? Let me see God. Let me feel God, not personal opinions and natural eye breakdowns that serve no purpose.

Some traditions are made to be broken because times change. We were taught God never changes, which I do believe. However, we as human beings must evolve; so, change is needed. Yet "God never changes" was a way of saying neither does tradition. If that were the case, we would not now have in the United States of America more women working and advancing their careers or Barack Obama as former president of the US of A.

A force also existed to hold as fact, the head clergy's interpretation of the King James Bible. Different understandings from that of the head clergy on a particular scripture were openly ridiculed or dismissed. Thinking for ourselves only to find conflict within understanding was being rebellious. We were rebutted particularly when we applied scripture to contest some of the ways of the head clergy, which some viewed as living life in contradiction of the teachings. Such a controlled environment leads to closed-minded persons. Perhaps that was the point.

Not everyone's complete interpretation of any book or the Bible is the same. Generally, some differences of opinion will exist. Sometimes it takes multiple opinions to conclude. Sometimes it takes multiple opinions to agree to disagree.

A misconception exists that church goers have to be perfect or overly disciplined, also known as being uptight. All human beings should try for self-discipline, but there is no perfect kind of human being. We should accept our flaws and work on them, should we choose.

CHAPTER 5:

Say What!

C ARNAL minded? Let's evaluate. If you saw multiple women constantly accompanying a clergy member, who happened to be married, and asked questions in rebuttal of this behavior and consequently were told that you were carnal minded, how would you react? I tell you, the words, *WHAT IN THE WORLD*, come to mind. For those who may not know the definition of *carnal*, it basically means "fleshly." In other words, the underlying issue is that the objector's fleshly thinking is getting in the way of the spiritual picture; and only a person with a spiritual eye can understand the *godly* purpose of being accompanied by multiple women.

If we are taught one thing but see another, asking a question in expectation of a reasonable answer is only right. We all have natural eyes with which some of us are blessed to see. It does not take a spiritual eye to connect certain dots to come to a reasonable conclusion.

This is the type of behavior that will cause someone to no longer attend church. Contrary to what I was taught, leaving the church is not leaving God. However, some people have experienced so much hurt by members of a particular church body that they have lost their belief in God. The result is they will never return to a church building.

Let me reassure that there is a difference between believing in a church and believing in God. The expectation of a church is that God will be at the forefront of the operation. When we see otherwise, we tend to lean towards the notion that there can't possibly be a God because *some* of the very people in the church claiming to have the closest relationship to God often do not properly represent God. This is where our personal relationship with God comes into focus. If we do not have one and base the existence of God solely on what we see from *some* church members, we are vulnerable to not believing.

We will always have shortcomings that may not be godly behavior, but I speak of habitual ways intended to maliciously degrade and tear down an individual. I, at one point, questioned God's existence. Believing because someone said there is a God and knowing because we've experienced God is not comparable. I know there is a God because of my personal experiences with God.

Looking up to human beings to the point that they seem infallible is not a good vantage point. Being open minded to the faults of human beings, no matter their titles, will leave room for more reasonable conclusions about who people really are. It allows for better judgment of character. Seeing people for who they are, not as they portray themselves or who we would like for them to be, leaves more room for understanding revealed imperfections.

The most significant human emotion missing from many churches is the expression of *love*. Sometimes love is gentle, sweet, and kind. Sometimes love is tough and stern but still effective and accepted as such, even if it takes time for one to realize its nature. Love is genuine. Love is unconditional. There is no mystery to love because it is pure and easy to see and feel.

I've witnessed personal wars inside of the church to the point that fuming feelings penetrated across the pulpit into a spectacle of anger and rage expressed in the person's sermon. The attack would be aimed at a person or a group of people who were not in agreement or would not comply, whether on a personal or so-called spiritual level.

Human emotions overwhelmingly reacted to situations, when then spilled over into the pulpit. Reasonable communication was not an option because unreasonable conclusions were often the source for this biased behavior. Public humiliation seemed to be the purpose for such outlandish behavior.

I've witnessed visitors walk into a church just to become victims of someone's sermon because they did not look up to the standard. Where is the love or God in such prejudging, ignorant behavior? I'll take it further: Where is the reasonably minded human-being? Everything is not so profound that it is a divine message. I do believe that everything happens for a reason, so we must be careful in the treatment of others because life happens. But some people overuse religious beliefs to mask personal views or their real persona as human beings.

Sin is defined as committing an act against divine law. That speaks for itself. Are any of us without sin or shortcomings? No. Sometimes people may take things personally because they feel someone has committed wrong against them. They then turn it around by saying the person committed a sin and use it as ammunition to defame the person across the pulpit, admonishing the individual to repent and ask for forgiveness. Forgiveness from whom and for what reason? It takes one person to forgive.

Misunderstandings that occur between individuals require perfection of effective forms of communication. The method of delivery in communicating a misunderstanding can have a tremendous impact on the outcome of acceptance. Screaming, yelling, or "rebuking" someone may not be the best method. A delivery with love, patience, understanding, and kindness tends to be a more welcomed approach: "And if I have prophecy and know all mysteries and all knowledge, and if I have all faith so as to remove mountains, but I do not have love, I am nothing" (1 Cor.13:2 DLNT).

CHAPTER 6:

Why Can't I Date and Why Do You Have to Choose My Mate?

Now we come to dating, with the biblical term of courting. Traditionally, we all know how this goes. A man and woman become interested in one another and go out on dates. Then, if they see fit, they get married, move in together, have children, and so forth.

I love the dating part of this model because it helps us know people better. But you guessed it, in my upbringing, dating was not permitted. Even if adults saw individuals with whom they shared mutual interests, they were forbidden to date. Anyone considered as a spousal option had to come from within the same church body, and only minimal one-on-one interaction was allowed. A premarital counseling session or two from the head clergy was sufficient to determine if the marriage would solidify.

With divorce at such a high rate today and the word itself being completely dismissed as an option because of some religious beliefs, once in an unhappy marriage, where is one to go if marriage vows are continually breached? I was taught to separate and "put away" your spouse. Then what? Is one to spend the remainder of life separated or unhappily married while waiting for the person to change?

More careful planning in choosing a spouse can avoid a lot of future turmoil. Nothing is definite, and we will experience hard times. However, one should know certain things about a person before committing to spending the rest of one's life with the individual, especially if divorce is not an option.

To this point, I am unmarried, so I am unsure what I would do if I ran into a situation where, after exhausting all possibilities, the marriage was insoluble. I do know I'd refuse to be unhappy because I felt trapped by tyrant behavior. Sometimes the best resolve is to dissolve.

I was raised to believe that the man is the head of the household. Of that I am in acceptance. But if the head of our household is not living up to the responsibility, we as individuals should take charge of life, not allowing tyranny because of tradition. Unfortunately, we now live in a society where more and more single mothers work and run their homes alone. How's that for breaking tradition? You have to do what you have to do. I am reminded of a familiar quote: "Someone else's happiness should not come at the expense of yours."

Perhaps a poll on how many married couples within the church are following the traditional way of marriage where the man goes out to work and the woman stays home to keep the house can be conducted. Nowadays, in most instances, it takes two to run a household, which most of the church world seems to have accepted. But, for whatever reason, other traditional values remain unbending.

If it is opposition to interact with the opposite sex or to, by a certain age, be allowed to date, how is one to get to know the general characteristics of male or female? From male or female figures in the family? I have six brothers and I come from a nuclear family, so that has helped immensely. However, setting reasonable age limitations for dating is more acceptable than ignoring the reality that it will eventually occur.

At a point, it's healthy to allow teenagers to date, or perhaps just friends of the opposite sex with which to communicate. This helps to develop life's social and emotional skills. All of this, of course, should be at the discretion of the parent because some gray areas exist when it comes to the topic of teenage dating. To my point, parents may be able to better teach their child while living in the home how to cope with dating. In turn, when children are on their own, they are more aware. Once children move out of the nest, they may not always use the dating advice they've been given; but, at least, parents should feel better about having shared their knowledge on the subject.

I really didn't develop a deep interest in boys until I was in high school. Before then, I had a few crushes but nobody I particularly wanted to make my boyfriend. Being hard to get was my natural persona. I inherited this trait from my mother. My mother always taught me to be independent. As I matured, I dated a lot and had fun doing so.

I recall, at age eighteen, asking my father's permission to go to my high school senior prom. His reply was that the dance was of the world. Okay, no problem. My prom happened to be on a church night, so I began to strategize with my older brothers and sisters as we improvised a way for me to attend.

First on the agenda was for me to call the guy I had had a crush on for years and ask him if he would accompany me to the prom. He didn't attend the same school at the time, so I had to swallow a pill and ask him instead of vice versa. Luckily, he said yes. Next, my sisters helped me find a dress and accessories. My sisters were animated about helping because they had not had the opportunity to attend their senior proms. I was blessed to have older sisters who understood and who were willing to help. My brothers helped my prom date pick out his suit and accessories. One allowed us to use his vehicle, driven by one of my sisters who was kind enough to chauffeur us to the prom. It was a team effort!

What was an even bolder move was my decision to stay out that night. After getting together with a few friends, I went to my sister's for the night. Although I walked into the dreaded disaster of someone else showing up with the same dress (Oh, no!), prom night was awesome!

The following day, I attended a church event wearing my praise shoes! Refreshed from prom night, I stood clapping and singing, which, at that point, was an abnormality. At one point, my father and I shared eye contact for a moment. It is a wonder he never mentioned anything to me about it, but I think he knew of my whereabouts the prior evening.

In my more serious relationships, I suffered severely with communicating certain thoughts or emotions concerning either the relationship or myself. I think we all sometimes have this issue, but part of my reason was because growing up I was not welcomed with open arms to discuss dating with my father. Thankfully, boys were a topic I could openly discuss with my mother as well as my sisters.

If I even mentioned a boy to my father, I heard, "We don't believe in boyfriends or girlfriends." I had always been given the impression that any opposing views would lead to confrontation or would be denied without consideration. Sometimes this mentality translated into my relationships, so the result was for me to simply cold shoulder an issue or speak arrogantly of it with a closed mind. Today, I've accepted these flaws and work on them daily, with evidence of immense improvement.

CHAPTER 7:

Am I Giving Too Much Money Away?

T ITHES and offerings were a hot topic of discussion. Most churches, including my former, follow scriptural guidance in giving ten percent of earnings towards tithing, with offerings coming as a separate giving. Scripture supports giving ten percent of any increase towards tithing, with whatever one may have left to give being contributed towards offerings. Growing up, I did not fully understand the logic in this because many who practiced this formula seemed to struggle financially.

As I grew older, I gained an understanding from reading other books written by some of the most successful individuals—books that helped to enlighten me that God, who is the ultimate boss, permitted the most generous commission split. I do not know of any other boss who will allow me to keep ninety percent of my earnings. It is God that allows us to receive such earnings, so why not give the remaining ten percent of earnings towards tithes if possible?

Besides, churches need to pay bills in order to keep operating: light bills, gas bills, salaries, and so forth. To keep churches functioning, some form of membership payment should be made. Some churches have this fee separate from tithing and offerings.

During my tenure, members not giving ten percent for tithes was a negative thing. Individual circumstance at a given time may not liberate some people to give ten percent due to other personal financial commitments. Is giving less than ten percent due to such financial obligations, such as bills, food, insurance payments, and so forth, a bad thing considering one's heart's desire to do so once financial conditions improve? Better yet, what if some just choose not to give any percentage because they feel the government takes more than enough in taxes? To give or not to give is a personal choice.

I am a believer of charity beginning at home. Giving ten percent of earnings towards tithes is something I try to do, whether it is to my parents or family, a reputable charity, a church, or other worthy cause. I do not limit my giving to a church building, especially considering I do not belong to one. But, if for whatever reason I do not have ten percent of my earnings to give, I donate what I can in hope of being able to do better the next time around. When I do not have ten percent of earnings to donate, I try to ensure that I provide intangibles such as time and care for certain individuals or organizations.

I do not believe that tithing always has to be in monetary form. However, if a person can give ten percent or at least some earnings without facing financial hardship, I suggest you do so because I've seen, as well as experienced, that charitable giving is a formula for financial success, even if it is experienced in the long run. Hopefully, we position ourselves for better financial gain so donating ten percent comes more easily, without it being too much of a sacrifice that may expose us to financial hardships.

The following explains how I came to determine that being able to give ten percent of earnings is a process: One day while thinking on giving ten percent of my earnings to a reputable cause, I asked myself what would happen if I did not have the ten percent to give. Not long after, I walked into a place of business. There, a lady on television was speaking of tithing. She had once before struggled with the same question. She was just starting a business but could not give the full ten percent as desired. She stated God told her to just give what she could. She started with giving a smaller percentage of her earnings, which I believe was five percent. Shortly after giving the smaller percentage, she noticed her business start to pick up. It eventually came to the point where she was able to give her desired ten percent. Thereafter, business started to boom! That was my answer and I received it as such.

CHAPTER 8:

Tune Me In

I LOVE music in its healing mechanism. Let's test your, the reader's, knowledge of R&B throwbacks. Does "early one Sunday morning breakfast was on the table" sound familiar? It is a line to a throwback R&B song remixed by R. Kelly called "Sadie," a song that I first heard being chorused by my fifth-grade peers while on a school trip. Everyone I knew was participating. Well, everyone but me, because I didn't know the words. However, that didn't last too long as I quickly learned and joined in.

Why did I not know the words to the song? Because I was not allowed to listen to anything outside of the gospel station. I loved—and still do love—gospel music. It can be very inspiring and encouraging. However, sometimes certain gospel songs sound too depressing or just too extravagant. What's more, sometimes some music found outside of the gospel genre is just as inspiring and encouraging. This fact I was unaware of, until I started to cautiously listen with my earphones to the FM station on a regular basis, which back then, did not play gospel music.

Before that, I had a misconception that all music not on a gospel station was bad or profane. Listening to that type of music would corrupt my mind into possibly behaving as the music suggested.

Most of us can agree that no one would like a loved one, particularly an impressionable child, listening to certain music because of the potential negative impact. The same goes for certain movies under parental control to protect children from being exposed to certain visuals. But gospel singers who I do still listen to and love are not the only ones to compose and sing inspirational songs of love, hope, peace, and gratitude.

The main reason we were taught not to listen to any music outside of the gospel station was because those songs more likely did not mention the name of Jesus or God. If a song expresses genuine love (not lust) or positive inspiration, isn't that an expression of God? I needed to hear empowering songs in general, no matter the composer or the station. I listened to many songs on the FM station when coming home from a hard day at school or needing a mental break that provided much relief. Other times, I listened to boogie down music and got down!

Going to the movies, skating, or bowling, and playing pool was also off limits as they were viewed as doing things of the world. If members were known to be doing these things or allowed their children, an order of repentance was nigh. During my time, only a select few promoted attending college. I am appreciative of those few who did provide encouragement.

As children, my mother did not deprive us from school trips that involved skating, movies, bowling, and so forth. We were also blessed to be able to travel and to go on church and family trips, which is why I believe I still love to travel and enjoy adventure today.

Let's play another game called charades (in book form). I don't have any pictures for view, but I'll try to be as precise in detail as possible. I will describe two different scenes I've witnessed, and I would like for you, the reader, to try to decipher between the scenery of *some* churches and of clubs. The following character names are totally fictitious. Here we go!

Scene 1: John Doe is smoothed out in his best outfit, ready to get down and dance! John Doe pays at the door. John Doe walks in looking to see who has a better outfit. Other people look John Doe up and down then whisper to one another. John Doe thinks the music is a little dead, so he is waiting for the right song to come on. A popular song comes on, so everyone hits the dance floor. Oh, boy, only two people left on the dance floor. It's a dance off! The MC comes over the microphone to say it's time to settle down.

Scene 2: Jane Doe is pressed out in her best outfit ready to get down and dance! Jane Doe walks in looking to see who has a better outfit. Other people look Jane Doe up and down then whisper to one another. Jane Doe thinks the music is a little dead, so she is waiting for the right song to come on. An uplifting song comes on, so everyone hits the dance floor. Oh, boy, only two people left on the dance floor. It's a dance off! The MC comes over the microphone to let everyone know it's time to bring it in for tithes and offering.

From the two descriptions, you were probably able from key words to decipher the scenery at *some* churches and at clubs. I italicized the word *some* to be sure not to stereotype and to emphasize that all churches are not the same. Some make it a priority to worship God in spirit and truth: "Let everything that hath breath praise the Lord" (Ps. 150:6 KJV). This goes from the birds that sing to the humans who worship. The key is "in spirit" and in "*truth.*" Looking good while praising God is awesome. Just be sure it's not about showcasing an outfit or outperforming the next individual. Dancing over issues one refuses to address and making amends doesn't make them disappear. It's temporary relief, but we still have to work toward resolution.

Sometimes we may need help to welcome God's spirit due to us not knowing how to do so or to being so weak we need the help of others to do so. Although some may pretend to be in connection with the spirit of God, the entire time, it is self or another person in operation. We should not be fooled or scared into thinking that God's spirit is in operation every time individuals are dancing in church or saying God gave them a vision. We should get to know God personally so we will be able to better determine. Anyone can dance on cue. I personally think a lot of times people dance out of formality. Going to church to worship God without dancing is fine.

CHAPTER 9:

To Sue or Not to Sue

A NOTHER belief was members were not to bring suit or testify in a court of law against each other under any circumstances. I do not recall which scripture was connected to this, but I do recall not agreeing with its interpretation. We do live in an overly litigious society, but certain acts require the legal system to settle if reconciliation between two parties is otherwise unachievable, resulting in the need for a mediator. Suing someone's insurance company to settle compensation for damages should not be one's preference; but if someone damages the property of another, seeking payment from a third party such as an insurance company to rectify the ordeal is reasonable. If someone does not have insurance, suing may be viewed as not only heartless but possibly pointless.

After no longer being a regular attender of church, I was involved in a money scam that involved a clergy member. When this occurred, I was in my early twenties. Because of the trust I had in this individual, I believed in the delivery of a promised specified amount of funds even when details of the business transaction did not align.

Long story short, even after the clergy member allegedly discovered the business venture was a scam from the beginning, I was still being misled to believe that an ensuing lump sum amount returning a significant profit on the initial investment was imminent. I sent monies on several occasions based on the trust and word of the individual. I found out from another investor that it was a scam, but the clergy member did not disclose this information. After confrontation and a demand for the return of my initial investment, I received *most* of the monies and decided not to seek further recourse to recoup the remainder.

Another investor who had not received any repayment tried for years to reconcile the differences just between the two parties. Unfortunately, after many broken promises from the clergy member to return the initial investment and the word "brother" being used by the clergy member to prevent the commencement of a lawsuit, the investor finally filed suit.

For anyone to treat someone wrongly then to attempt to use manipulative Bible verse tactics to escape ownership of such a wrong is just simply *wrong*. Taking advantage of an individual is not something any human should do to another in expectance of escape. What goes around comes around, but it tends to come back around more viciously. It's just a rule of life I've come to know personally. God's grace and mercy surely come in handy when life decides to return a favor that's not so favorable.

CHAPTER 10:

Humble or Cowardly?

W HAT is being humble? This term was often used when someone in authority wanted the cooperation of another. I often
encountered conversation where I would have a question regarding interpretation of a scripture or just an opinion of another. When
an explanation which I might not agree with was provided, I might
have remained persistent with my thoughts. At that point, I was told
I needed to humble myself, that I was spiritually blind and should ask
God to open my eyes to an understanding. I beg your pardon?

The reason for this advice was that Jesus was humble and modest,
so I needed to follow in his footsteps. Jesus was so much more than
we will ever know. To use this one characteristic of Jesus to persuade
an individual to give in to a dictatorship is absurd; but questioning a
leader within the church was thoroughly frowned upon.

For example, we were not allowed to wear opened-toe shoes/
sandals. One day I asked why it was not allowed. The response was that
men were attracted to feet so exposure of the feet would create lustful

thoughts. My response to that was, "Men are attracted to everything. You could be covered from head to toe and some would still wonder what is underneath." I was also told that it provided too much exposure of the body. When I questioned that, as far as I perceived, I did not receive a reasonable answer.

Under certain circumstances, being humble is fine; but knowing the difference between being humble and being cowardly is very important. As adults, if we feel belittled due to listening to advice we prefer not to follow and then, on top of that, do not ask any questions, we are not being humble. We are being cowardly. We do not have to speak up on everything on which we disagree, but it is worth the effort in protecting self-respect.

I was also taught to not question God. At times I needed to know the answers to some things that individuals were not able to provide, so I asked God, who did provide answers. How is it not possible for us as children of God to not be able to ask God a question? I understand what God says is final, but I also understand God provides answers to questions we may not otherwise understand.

To me, a picture was painted that if we struggle here on earth, our reward will be provided in heaven during the afterlife. I too have that hope of having a better afterlife, but waiting for that to occur to get a piece of the pie is a lazy-possessed mentality. One does not have to struggle here on earth, and one does not have to wait to die to receive certain things. A form of heaven on earth can be experienced now.

Overcoming struggles was too often recited rather than avoiding certain struggles in the first place by exercising faith that maneuvers us into a better position in life. Poor decision making usually leads to poor outcomes. Some struggles are certainly inevitable, but others are avoidable just the same.

Patience is a virtue, which is certainly true. Conversely, using this phrase to avoid handling responsibility, such as gaining employment, is a show of lazy behavior. We may have to wait for things in trying our faith, but others we have the capacity to act on by setting reasonable time limitations for achievement. "I'm just waiting on the Lord" is a mentality that should diminish.

When I attended church on a regular basis, the word *rebuke* was often used. For instance, if individuals, particularly members, were known to have committed a sin or showed behavior contrary to the teachings, they were often rebuked. This might have come in the form of consecrated oil being laid on the head of the offender or a verbal public display of disapproval. The point was to "cast out" the hindrance or teach the person a lesson. If people showed objection to their rebuking, their targeted "demons" were speaking out. Although this was possible, sometimes I personally thought these persons were angry at the demonstration and so expressed their emotions.

What happened if these persons just sat there in disgust? They could be subject to long sessions, if not all night, of prayer. Have you ever seen an individual being forced to call on Jesus while being angry? Not a pretty picture. The name of Jesus should be called upon freely, with dignity and respect.

I find it interesting that some believe a rebuking is a mystic (for lack of a better word or phrase) experience that will make a person change certain habits or characteristics. If people see no wrong in what they are doing and therefore do not care to change, all the rebuking in the world will not change those individuals. Even if the behavior temporarily ceases, it will shortly be resumed. In fact, sometimes rebuking just angers the person, not the so-called demon.

I've witnessed some forceful rebuking in a church that revealed personal, not spiritual, objectives. In other words, the ones administering the rebuking only did so because of a personal vendetta they had against the person.

You be the judge. One places "consecrated" oil on one's hand, winds up (hand and arm going back), then without warning, places the opened hand on the head of an individual which, due to the aggression, forces the individual's head back. This is followed with a reciting of words said to allegedly release the demon. Would that make the average person angry? On a few occasions, I thought a fight had broken out during church service; but it was just someone being rebuked.

I do believe in the power of prayer, but the receiver has to be in position to receive such an experience. Trying to personally cast out a demon is not something self should take on. Allowing the spirit of God to guide us in doing so is advisable. Every sin or habit should not be classified as a demon. Putting personal feelings on the back burner will eliminate a lot of the rebuking occurring in some churches.

Ego can get in the way of God's mission. Learning to put ourselves in another person's shoes can help purge selfish behavior that is blind to some realities. Usually, people who possess big egos are easily angered when they feel they are not being obeyed. Big egos possessed by human beings tend to blind God's purpose. Personal opinions are always mixed with the ultimate will of God. God's will should be the will of man. A man's will is different in nature. Hopefully, we align with God's purpose designed for each of us as unique individuals. A little ego is always good for a person, but too much of one leads to arrogance that carries ignorance.

A lot of talent was wasted because of wide-spread favoritism. Personal feelings sometimes got in the way of the bigger spiritual picture. Certain individuals loved the spotlight and stopped at nothing to acquire such, even at the expense of their own humiliation.

Backbiting, also known as bad-mouthing, is defined as malicious talk about someone who is not present. This was a blistering discussion during more than enough sermons. Basically, church members who allegedly spoke against other church members outside of their presence were said to have committed a sin.

If we feel or see someone do something incorrectly and we share that with someone outside of their presence, where is the wrong in that? Particularly if an attempt to resolve the issue with the perpetrator had already occurred? For example, a loved one who attended the church might mention to a third party out of frustration that something had happened within the church or with a church member. According to some, this qualified as backbiting.

Okay, so let me explain what would happen using the other approach where individuals might go to a clergy member or other church member to explain in a respectful manner how they were offended by something the individual may have done. That too was sometimes mentioned from the pulpit. The clergy member or individual used to actually come out and say, "I had someone come to me saying, ..." What happened to the confidentiality or trust? What was the point of mentioning it from the pulpit? To deter someone from approaching a potential future issue or to humiliate?

In an effort to protect the privacy, confidentiality, and security of certain information within churches, organizations, government entities, and so forth, some precautionary measures should be taken. However, personal issues are another issue. Because it is personal, that information can be disclosed with whomever the offended may feel comfortable sharing, even if not with the source. The hope is that it can first, if safe conditions allow, be shared with the offender in a confidential, resolute manner.

The more people we have trying to come to agreement, the more struggle we will encounter. If at a point we express our frustration with an individual to someone else, is that backbiting? On a professional level, counselors deal with this daily. Should they tell their clients to stop backbiting against whomever?

Discussing differences in general in which one may be involved should not be considered gossiping or backbiting.

CHAPTER 11:

A Let Down Because
of a Come Up

Too often, displays of jealousy occurred for what others may have gained, such as a new car, a new house, or perhaps a spouse. "Love thy neighbor as you love yourself" was out the window, and sermons directly connected to the perceived benefit were suddenly rendered in protest of the same, without thought as to what these individuals may have gone through to attain their material possessions. More to it, every blessing received does not have to be the result of struggle; it may simply be favor. What happened to just being happy for someone and learning how to accomplish the same should one desire to do so?

Getting what was viewed by most to be a finer car or dressing "better" than someone during a service invaded enough sermons to the point that some saw acquiring the finer things in life as adversarial. Having finer things was an indication of a carnal mind that subjected individuals to believe they were better than others. One could look forward to becoming a bullseye because the darts would surely be thrown.

God blessing individuals to be able to acquire the finer things in life does not mean they have to think they are better than others because they simply aren't. The same God who gives can surely take away. The perception that people may think they are better than others because they seem to be better off in one way or another is an imprinted misconception possessed by some human beings, a misconception that shelters the underlying issue of jealousy. In fact, some believe that they are better than others for whatever reasons. But to automatically put everyone into this classification because of their material gain is not only judgmental but also hypocritical. Plenty of people carry material gain with *class*.

CHAPTER 12:

Give Me Freedom

So many rules and regulations rob people of freedom. Walking on eggshells not fully enjoying life is not the way human beings should live. The impression to live such a dull and strict path is the reason that, when clergy or church members are known to have committed a wrong, they are persecuted by humans to the maximum level. The picture of being perfect is so painted that when imperfection is exposed, forgiveness from individuals is a rarity. Relating person to person daily and not hiding behind scriptural text will help people to better understand mistakes.

Having authority control so much of one's life deprives one of individualism. The misconception exists that the best cannot be experienced here on earth. Can we not experience peace, joy, love, happiness, good health, wealth, fun, prosperity, and so forth right now? Yes.

Where are we going as a human race when people find more love, grace, and freedom outside of the four walls of a church building? Because we all do not look alike, dress alike, breathe alike, or think alike, certain ones are said to be doomed for eternal damnation. When did God designate man to decide the final fate of any human being? It's time to get over whatever perceived advantage we may think we have over others because *we say* we are followers of God when we may *show* just the opposite. No human being is better than the next under any circumstances. With maturity, we may develop the ability to prevent putting ourselves in certain situations; but it doesn't make us any better than the next person.

Some happily support religion, as do I when it is correctly organized. Some reputable leaders of religion deserve commending. In my adult life, I've visited some churches because I felt led by God and, in doing so, received from the sermon confirmation of God-sent messages. Some churches can put aside personal biases and deliver messages of love and hope. Some religions do, in fact, abide by what is fair as well as by what is reasonably surmised according to scriptural text and human morals. I can only tell you of some of my personal experiences.

In the beginning of this section, I gave my personal interpretation of religion. Now I will give one of its definitions: "the belief in and worship of a superhuman controlling power, especially a personal God or gods." One more definition I feel compelled to share is that of the word *cult*: "a relatively small group of people having religious beliefs or practices regarded by others as strange or sinister." You be the judge. ☺

In the next chapter, we move to another level of devotion that deals with complete mind control of another: *brainwashing*.

PART II

WHEN RELIGIOUS PRACTICES
TURN INTO BRAINWASHING

CHAPTER 13:

Brainwashing in the Works

THE definition of brainwashing is making someone adopt radically different beliefs by using systematic and often forcible pressure.

To a degree, I understand that religion comes with a set of beliefs and rules that believers of each should follow and that certain levels of control are necessary to maintain structure in any organization. Such control levels are not only necessary but also healthy. However, excessive control becomes crippling.

For example, in a relationship, one has a structured set of guidelines to follow to contribute to its success or detriment. I think more than enough people can agree that effective communication is one of the most pertinent parts of a relationship. Perhaps one person in each relationship is better at communicating and the other is better with finances. The one who is stronger in an area may control that aspect of the relationship, while the other controls that person's particular stronger suit. By control, I mean being the dominant but reasonable leader in a particular skill who does not mind teaching it should the other desire to learn. It takes a team to run any business or relationship. However, ones who may be better at a given skill can easily be negatively influenced by their significant others should they allow it.

Where am I going with this? To tell you the truth, for a minute I didn't know. ☺ But to my point, neither one of the persons in the relationship should dominate to the point that the other does not think on their own or does not voice their opinions, even though they are entitled to do so. If domination takes place, one voice is lost because the other voice speaks on its behalf. Sooner or later the person who is being dominated feels their opinion is worthless. The person then starts to depend on their significant other more readily.

Ultimately, such domination harms not only the relationship but also the unique individualism each person possesses. Low self-esteem then penetrates, causing the mind to be more vulnerable to control to the point that thinking for self is subdued by what we believe our significant other would like best. Then we act accordingly.

As time goes on in following the same formula, our thoughts are eventually controlled and possessed by another. We've surrendered our thoughts and adopted theirs. We feel we need the person because we've relied on them so heavily. Our mentality is to please that person even if we feel they may be wrong. Sometimes we may be aware of the person's wrong and want to speak up; but because we seek their approval, we keep as silent as a defenseless child.

I've witnessed mind manipulation in the religious sector being used to the point of insanity. At this level, religious beliefs are camouflaged, no longer playing a significant role. The written doctrine or Bible is used as a manipulating tool to control others to fulfill self-gratification. This results in the adoption of someone else's beliefs which are worshipped to their core. It causes us to neglect our family, friends, and, most importantly, God.

From what I've witnessed, the difference between this level and religion is that religion is a set of rules and beliefs followed and believed by the followers of that religion. The rules apply to everyone and are based strictly on written doctrine, which dictates such behavior. Anyone found out of compliance is viewed as behaving incorrectly, subjecting one to potential consequence.

On the other hand, at the brainwashing level, religion is intentionally used to control people's minds. Such control can easily include personal objectives and opinions that fulfill self-purposes such as money, sex, lies, power, and the like. The beliefs or rules apply at the convenience of one dominating source who enforces these beliefs and who applies word games to scriptural text to maintain a certain level of controlled thinking.

The most significant emotion used as leverage at this level is *fear*. The manipulator or clergy applies fear tactics backed by a false interpretation of a doctrine to the congregation or individual to ensure a certain level of control is maintained. If such persons feel that level of control is threatened, they concoct a strategy to overthrow the "bad apple."

What are the possible strategies? I've witnessed a person being openly ridiculed continuously from the pulpit and called an anti-Christ just because, in private, the individual expressed opposition with a clergy. The congregation was then advised to *stay away* from said individual as the person was covered by the wrong spirit. Otherwise, we could be on our way to hell right along with them.

Did people listen? You better believe it. The reasoning was that "they just wanted to be saved." In church, I seemed to hear the word *hell* so many more times than *heaven*. The end result was the accused "anti-Christ" felt isolated and so asked for forgiveness, even when feeling the individual was correct. Of course, the word used to describe this backing down was "humble." At times, these persons were commended for showing "humbleness"; other times, mercy was not so readily given. (I can think of a word or two that doesn't exactly fit the definition of humble.) Some stayed. Others had the courage to leave. Why would someone put up with this behavior? Because they *feared* going to hell from being disobedient to their leader.

I do believe we should try to avoid going to a place for eternity believed to be filled with fire and brimstone. However, the energy and focus should not be on the avoidance of such damnation but on the hope of making it to a better place in the afterlife. Some simply do not believe there is a heaven or hell. Who am I to contest their belief? My belief is not up for debate, so why should I care to debate others? I do believe we can experience a form of hell and heaven right here on earth. Let me be clear: I said a "form" of heaven and a "form" of hell.

The fear of God is one thing, but the fear of individuals who say they know God is totally different. At this level, these people use their titles fully as leverage. The higher the title, the more leverage to convince others that the entitled is the only one to receive messages from God that others are not privileged to hear. Yet, coincidentally, the messages always pertain to how someone else needs to get it right. Every personal objective is camouflaged in the context of the Bible. There's always some type of word twist or manipulation of the truth to accommodate the entitled one's personal desires or opinions. The only concern is control, not the soul.

One day as one of my loved ones struggling with end stage renal disease was being admitted into the hospital, I was greeted by a familiar church clergy who insisted I could not get a prayer through to help my loved one because I wasn't "saved." The scripture used for this was, "Now we know that God heareth not sinners: but if any man be a worshipper of God, and doeth his will, him he heareth" (John 9:31 KJV). Needless to say, I briskly brushed this off without a response because I was aware that God had already heard a plethora of my requests: The best truth is evidently seen. I was not persuaded into becoming a member of a particular church body so that God could hear my prayers, because, gratefully, God was already doing so. "Let he who is without sin cast the first stone." Let's just say I'm not ducking to dodge any stones.

How could a clergy member dare say that to a human being instead of "let's pray" and do this *together*? One reason I've personally witnessed is that these individuals are brainwashed.

CHAPTER 14:

Mind Games

THE intent of brainwashed individuals is not to hurt anyone's feelings. These individuals truly believe in what they are saying or doing, but it is one-sided, brainwashed thinking.

How does one get to this point in the religious sector? The predator in the form of God's servant uses kindness and warm gestures, as well as the special gifts provided to him or her from God, to lure individuals who may be in vulnerable situations. We all have gifts, and it is up to us how we put them to use. For example, if we have the gift of prophesy, we may use it in the church or in opening our own business as a fortune teller.

After helping an individual with a personal breakthrough, the predator uses it as never-ending leverage to manipulate the person into doing whatever the predator says God has instructed. At this point, these individuals feel compelled and obligated to the one who "helped" them get to a better place in life. They fail to understand it was the spirit of God provoked inside of them that helped with the breakthrough. The spirit of God can be called upon by anyone who is ready to welcome the presence, just as someone who is ready to receive will receive.

If the controlled tries to leave, predators activate the fear tactic. They use people's past lives before their personal breakthroughs against them to convince them that if they leave the church (also phrased as "turning their back on God"), they will not only return to that unfavorable lifestyle but also be worse off. As a result, even against their own will and God's, the devoted stay. In other words, "the man or woman of God told me, so I got to do as my leader says," not realizing that, in life, we are our own leaders and, if allowed, God will do the guiding.

As time passes, the clergy members or disguised servants of God can tell controlled individuals exactly what to do, when to do it, and how to do it. If these persons hear a word from God that is not in agreement with the controllers' objectives, the response is "God did not say that." In turn, without any objectivity, they accept that rebuttal. At this point, these men and women have become the controlled individuals' god.

I compare this process to a man who meets a woman who, in the beginning, concludes for whatever reason he has no real future with her but proceeds to use dishonesty and manipulation to gain control to get what he desires. Persuasion may be in the form of sending flowers, listening when a shoulder is needed, wining and dining, trips, and so forth. (Then, again, it doesn't take much to persuade some nowadays, unfortunately.) After he feels comfortable, the real person surfaces and starts to control/manipulate the woman even further.

By then, the woman is already vulnerable and softened so that the heart, not the mind, starts to dominate her decision making. She is vulnerable for him, and the man recognizes such. He can do no wrong; and even if he does, the woman makes excuses on his behalf. The woman stays even knowing she is being taken advantage of as the flowers, wining and dining, and trips are replaced with lying, cheating, verbal and sometimes physical abuse, empty pockets, and so on. Although the woman does not feel her true self-worth, it becomes difficult to break loose because her emotions are deeply involved.

Not all men behave in this manipulating manner. Some are genuine in their intent in satisfying a woman, so please be sure not to stereotype kind behavior from a man as a manipulative tactic, because a woman should be treated as such. Similarly, not all clergy members abuse power. Learning to distinguish a person's motives may take a little time; patience is required to determine them. Even when things seem all figured out, sometimes an unexpected turn of events occurs that changes the entire dynamic of a relationship.

I hope this example between a man and a woman provided better clarity.

I believe an intentional division was imposed within my family. The main objective of those looking to control others' minds is to ensure their voices are listened to as supreme regardless of any other thoughts, including personal, families', friends', and God's. That is their way to gain maximum control without threat. This can cause chaos within the family when just even one out of numerous family members is blind.

How does one leave one's family member in the emergency room to attend a church service? Easily when brainwashed. At this point, missing service is viewed as letting down the "servant" of God who happens to be their leader. Such individuals don't want to do that because they're afraid of the consequences. Again, everything stated by the controllers must be true because they are looked at as God.

Occasionally, when some individuals missed church services without "legitimate" reasons, they were subject to open rebuking in front of the entire congregation. How humiliating! Or maybe that was the point.

Brainwashing is a game being played with minds to continually demonstrate proven authority through relentless control. Controlled persons ultimately have ultimate faith that the controllers can do no wrong and so adhere to every word of their advice. The controllers use the love of God these weaker persons have against them as they wish to please God. These individuals hope that pleasing the persons viewed as having shown them to God and, hopefully, to heaven suffices.

Some victims of this heinous behavior believe there is no way out because they *fear* so much of the unknown. They do not believe in themselves or in the full power of God they can personally experience.

I've always been one to believe in the power of prayer and unity. As a preacher's daughter, I did not understand how some claiming to be closest to God could display such hate and favoritism.

Feeling unaccepted because of not being a member of a particular church is a familiar feeling: the feeling and display of someone believing that they are better than the next because they attend a particular church building multiple times a week; the feeling of people looking down on others because some do not believe the same way. Who people in this mind frame think they are is beyond me as we are all made of flesh and blood. To think of ourselves as better than others reveals not religious or brainwashing issues but insecurity issues.

I recall being told of someone mentioning from the pulpit that one of my siblings and I dressed like whores. One would wonder why such a thing was stated, especially by a clergy member. Was this a display of love or part of a plan to a hidden agenda? What purpose did it serve in rendering God's word?

I'll answer and say not one. So, what was the point? To humiliate us or fulfill a personal agenda? (shoulder shrug)

Have you ever attempted to tell someone in a bad relationship with a no-good man or woman that the person deserves better or that you saw the individual's significant other with another? Was the result the person snapping at you or at the other woman or man but not at the culprit? This behavior is similar to what happened if someone mentioned a wrong, they were aware the head clergy of my former church had committed. First came an uproar of rebuttal, and we were told we better watch what we said about the servant of God. Yes, the words *what in the world* come back to mind, as well as *unbelievable*.

Meanwhile, as the head clergy advised others, continual evidence showed they were not following their own advice: saying to show love but expressing hate, saying to tell the truth but continually misleading, giving marriage counseling but being unable to keep theirs in check. However, even with knowledge of this behavior, people remained loyal. For what reason? Because of an abundance of fear.

Constantly hearing someone say "don't" and "won't" has a mental effect. It's like the person's voice constantly echoes inside of one's head and dictates every move made. This is precisely the point. Negative thoughts come often as one fears doing even the simplest things due to being scared to death of the consequences. For example, I know some are expecting negative things to happen to me for writing this book; but just the opposite shall occur, so keep waiting.

Death is used as a scare tactic and dying in sin is perpetuated as a result for those who do not listen. By that point, the controllers have manipulated the conscious and subconscious minds so that when the conscious speaks and the subconscious reacts, they mirror the thoughts of the controller. That little voice is mistaken as the voice of God; and without thought, the controllers program their movement so that they are almost robotic in nature. ☺

In a way, everything is "yes, master, I understand." It takes time and patience to learn the mind of an individual inside out as well as to persuade the person to adopt another way of thinking. But when accomplished, these individuals render complete control to someone who does not deserve to control any portion of anyone's life.

A programmed human voice is confused with the voice of God. At this level, individuals have difficulty distinguishing between the two because of blind loyalty to unworthy individuals who have intentionally brainwashed. When praying, some may even see the faces of their leaders as well as hear their voices in the back of their heads.

From personal experience, when praying, I try to not focus on a human being's face or voice but to develop a tranquil mental space that allows for a clear transmission from me to God that will allow God to eventually assist in the conversation. Other times, prayer is just a quick conversation that says, "God, thank you for another day." The key point for me is to have clarity so I can hear and feel the exchange when needed. Sometimes it takes a little to push through to get to that moment of clarity; other times it comes rather easily. I truly believe in the science of prayer. ☺

Thankfully, I never conformed totally to this type of dictatorship. Although young in age, I sensed something was wrong. Nevertheless, as the daughter of a clergy member, I was still subject to many rules and regulations, even more so than the average church member. Yet I did not become a product of such unreasonable thinking. The hardest struggle for me was releasing fear or guilt for doing the smallest things and my reliance on the opinions of others.

College opened my mind to different beliefs and philosophies I may have not otherwise been exposed to. Learning just a little about different religions and philosophies, such as Buddhism and Hinduism, helped me ascertain that being open minded about religion was okay. I didn't adopt many of these briefly studied beliefs, but it was good to be educated. In my opinion, the best spiritual education comes directly from God and life experiences.

CHAPTER 15:

No Wedding Bells

My loved ones missed many important occasions due to them having to attend church functions instead. Under no circumstances was anyone to attend important events such as graduation ceremonies if they conflicted with church scheduling. I recall some of my loved ones missing some of the more important moments of life, such as graduations and birthday celebrations, due to their church attendance requirement.

If someone, including a close loved one, was getting married but was not a member of that particular church body, the church members were forbidden to attend that wedding. This requirement applied to fathers, mothers, brothers, sisters, uncles, and so on, regardless of the night of the wedding ceremony. The basis for the absence requirement was the notion that attending such events would constitute compromising to things of the world. If not a part of that church body, one was "worldly."

Some may view missing special occasions of loved ones because another man or woman advised against attendance due to church obligations as selfish behavior. Those who still attended said ceremonies against the advice of their clergy members were ridiculed in front of the congregation for being disobedient.

Certain events happen once in a lifetime, and certain memories are lasting, whether good or bad. The impact of a loved one missing an important event, particularly that of a reliant child, is never good. Of course, at the brainwashing level, nothing matters but pleasing the controller. Everyone else can repeatedly suffer from the actions of the controlled; but as long as the controller is happy, the controlled always attempts to justify this person's questionable behavior.

CHAPTER 16:

Genuine Communication

O NE night while in service, one of my brothers professed God called him to preach. Shortly thereafter, a pulpit member followed up, advising that God did not call him to preach as proclaimed. If we are given a mission by God, we will know without doubt. If someone else does not understand, that's fine. My brother soon after joined another church body and, later on, became a very blessed elder. Yet, he didn't care much for the title, just for the mission.

When someone can completely control how one operates spiritually, that person impacts every aspect of the controlled individual's life, including the financial and personal. Had my sibling listened to what was denounced, he probably would not be as blessed as he is now, either on a spiritual or on a personal level. Listening to God is supreme, even when no one else understands or becomes jealous because of the relationship shared with God. But it is difficult to hear God's voice when so much negativity and distractions clutter one's mind.

To hear God and recognize the communication, our minds must be at a certain space. If it is not, God may send a message; but we may not recognize it or may completely ignore it. Every word received from God does not have to be shared with another individual. Some things are sacred and do not need to be shared if one does not desire to discuss it with a human being who may divulge such confidential information. What is of most importance is to learn the different forms of communication God uses to reach each of us as individuals. God uses multiple avenues for communication, so we should keep open minds.

Every communication will not come from the Bible. Signs are all around us, but please do not allow superstition to take over. That can become very stressful as it sometimes requires overthinking. God will send signs that are up to us to grasp. God works in mysterious ways. ☺

Once communication is established more regularly, it will become more recognizable. It is the same with any personal relationship. The more effectively we use communication, the easier it becomes to communicate with loved ones.

How can a clergy member operate as a pimp for generations with very little resistance against such behavior? I've witnessed women who did not cooperate with a clergy member's personal agenda only to be treated as peasants in front of the entire congregation, reducing them to tears. Why would someone put up with such verbal abuse? Because of the *fear* of *man*.

The hurt and pain, as well as a cry for help, was seen in these victims' eyes; but unfortunately, most of the time, the women were filled with so much fear and emotional turmoil that their defenseless mode conquered them. If they had spoken of certain acts committed by the clergy member, the congregation would more than likely have sided with the clergy because of their unwarranted trust in a human being appearing to be beyond certain behavior.

It is a shame to see abuse of power hidden behind a title. I've seen it at both professional and religious levels. Title, money, and power are used to lure targets. How a congregation can sit back and watch a vicious cycle repeat generation after generation destroying lives is unfathomable.

Fear of standing up for self and caring about what a human being says over what God expects of us result in a bad predicament. When our minds are not our own, a defenseless feeling subdues logic. At a point, we should care mostly about our personal perceptions of self, not about others' opinions. Hiding behind the name of God is getting old, and people are swiftly catching on.

CHAPTER 17:

Abuse of Power

B ECAUSE of the way most of us have been taught to deal with God, we have developed too much fear to get to know God personally. This is exposed in the way people fabricate hidden personal agendas by saying God told them something. Just the name God alone raises eyebrows and gets the attention of most, as it should. But if we separate the fear and respect, we have for the person from the fear and respect we have for God, we can make a better judgment call on the reliance of the message.

To better understand, we must develop a personal relationship with God so when God reveals our personal characteristics, our awareness is keen. Confirmation should come in one way or another, confirmation of an already known, which is always nice.

Open confession is good for the soul. Priest—penitent confidentiality? Much to the dismay of the sanctity in sharing confidential information with a clergy member, "open confession is good for the soul" was many times used to prod an individual to confess a "sin" in front of the congregation and ask for forgiveness. In fact, sometimes when the individual confided in a clergy member behind closed doors, the person was still advised to confess in front of the congregation.

At one time, openly confessing was abundant as some were made to feel guilty for doing the simplest things, such as playing pool or missing a service every now and again. Because disobedience to the regulations was disobeying authority, asking for forgiveness, as well as an order of repentance, was expected.

I remember a time I was told that all other churches were wrong. There seemed to be an ongoing campaign to ensure no one attended churches that were not part of that body without first getting consent. Key differences in diverse religious sectors were noted as being negative in nature. In fact, it was strongly suggested to not attend other churches period. Such behavior was strongly refuted, without compromise. We were told we could not leave the truth to find the truth. I say God is the truth; and wherever God is, there is truth, no matter the place.

Why not go elsewhere to fellowship? What's wrong with joining hand and hand with others to serve God. The goal should be to fulfill God's purpose. Controllers usually do not allow this, however, because it relinquishes power to another authority, which doesn't sit too well with them.

Forgiveness? According to my upbringing and the wonderful readings and teachings of Bishop T. D. Jakes in his book *Let It Go*, as well as others I've had the pleasure of indulging, forgiveness is a one-way street. I've personally experienced forgiving someone so I can agree. If it does not make sense to some, maybe this will better clarify. Sometimes we may offend someone and may not even know, so we do not apologize. However, it is up to the offended to let it go so that it does not sit in the heart, holding that person back from freedom. If it is of importance, the person may look to reveal that hurt and reconcile with the offender. However, it does not take reconciliation with the offender for the offended to forgive. Just the acts of releasing and self-reconciliation constitute forgiveness.

You see how easy this *can* be if one embraces the experience? However, forgiveness is sometimes a process because some hurt penetrates so deeply into the heart it is difficult and painful for us to let go or even identify the source of the hurt.

I've witnessed dictators continually order people they felt committed sins to go to the altar, repent of the wrong, and ask for forgiveness. After weeks—sometimes months—of the same purging, also known as spitting and sweating at the altar, these dictators suggested these individuals still needed to continue to ask God for forgiveness. Sometimes the dictators would just look down from the pulpit in an uncompassionate manner as these individuals sincerely requested God's forgiveness while tarrying at the altar.

How can clergy members behave in such a dictating manner when they themselves are doing worse? ☺ I'll tell you how: personal feelings, ego, and abuse of power. It was not that God had not forgiven these individuals; it was that the clergy members felt so violated by these persons breaking rules/regulations that not until they personally let it go could they relinquish it.

It does not take much for God to forgive. In fact, I believe forgiveness is based on the sincerity of the request. Sin, as well as mistakes, is a part of human nature; so, God expects us to pretty much screw up as it is part of our character.

Beating up ourselves for a sin someone else will not personally forgive is not wise. Having a relationship with God allows us to know when God renders forgiveness. Remember that forgiveness is a one-way street. We must also remember to forgive ourselves because often God has already done so before we even act. A person who refuses to forgive has a personal issue to resolve.

When we knowingly offend someone, hopefully, we are woman or man enough to apologize and never do the same. Sometimes hearing "I apologize" makes it easier to forgive, but the main responsibility lies in the hands of the offended to forgive. Being careful in the way we deal with ourselves and other humans is essential. Constantly treating a person wrong then asking for forgiveness is childish behavior immersed in a lack of self-control.

CHAPTER 18:

Is it Personal or Spiritual?

P ERSONAL conviction is not the same as God's conviction. A person can make us feel bad for doing something, but that doesn't equate to the conviction of God. That is an entirely different experience, one which, once beheld, will never again be confused.

A trick of personal conviction because of personal views was often used to make an individual feel so wrong and down for doing the littlest things, such as telling a joke (a.k.a. lying to someone) or going to a basketball game. One should ask, "Does God really see this as wrong?" The argument may be that disobedience to the leader is a sin; but it is not if one considers that God, who is the ultimate leader, allows it.

Time sometimes calls for someone to speak words of conviction that allow us to see a personal wrong we may not otherwise see as such, a conviction that humbles and opens the mind to a different and better perspective. These are human moments needed to help better our personal character. But where personal conviction is used to manipulate an adult into believing that a sin has been committed, causing one to feel horrible for the most miniscule movements that a reasonable adult would see as normal behavior, is more a matter of control rather than corrective action that leads to better future outcomes.

All the rules and regulations that came with serving a God who gives us free will to do so weighed heavily on that freedom. It robbed people of their unique individualism. How can one find purpose in life if their "leader" continues to dictate every portion of one's being? A great leader knows when to lead, when to follow, and when to let go.

With so many surrounding distractions during a service that could possibly occur, how can one fully tune in to show God attention? Isn't that the sole purpose of attending a church building? It seems some churches have become nothing more than reality TV shows, full of unnecessary drama that has nothing to do with God's objective.

So, if not God's objective, whose is being fulfilled? Is not enough genuine time given to properly serve God and learn God's purpose for each of us? To fulfill a position within a church just because someone told us is not wise. Knowing our purpose in life is up to each of us to discover, just the same as telling our father or mother, who may want us to become doctors, that we are instead going to become scientists. ☺

Countless lives of different races, genders, ages, creeds, and so on have been affected by ignorant behavior executed within the religious sector. During the composition of this book, I had the pleasure of speaking with a few people who were kind enough to share some of their personal experiences. The list included people of different ages, classes, genders, creeds, and races. Although different in characteristics and perhaps personalities, we all shared stories of similar experiences within the church, vividly recalled, which hurt us to the core. It is not an age, class, gender, creed, or race issue but a human issue.

In our next section, we focus on the transformation from religious and brainwashed thinking into the spirituality that allowed me to personally develop a better relationship with both self and with God.

PART III

SPIRITUALITY

CHAPTER 19:

Soothe My Broken Spirit

S PIRITUALITY is defined as a process of personal transformation either in accordance with traditional religious ideals or, increasingly, with subjective experience and psychological growth independent of any specific religious context.

Where do we turn when the very ones who undoubtedly assert to having a relationship with God and looking out for our best interests tear us down, build us up, and then tear us back down again? When they tell us *no* we can't or won't? When they put a cloud over dreams and visions because they do not conform with their own? When the mind is so enslaved with negativity we are no longer in control and negative thoughts bring forth negative realities? When we look for nonjudgmental delivery not based on personal views that ridicule because of personal appearance, decisions, or struggles? When we pay to keep the lights on instead of giving towards tithes or offerings on a given Sunday? When we're run out or kicked out of the home at an early age because we do not want to attend a church building but instead want to go to work or enroll in further education?

Our father? No, because he may be the source of some of the issues or may not be around. Our mother? No, there's only so much she can do because she is in love with or dependent on the man who is the source of some of the issues or is simply not around. Our brothers or sisters? No, because, if we have them, they too are damaged. People outside of the family? Perhaps, but they may not understand and may be just as confused about the situation. Even people who understand may not be upfront because they're afraid they may hurt our feelings. A significant other? No, because we've experienced hurt in previous relationships and do not care to share certain sides of ourselves. Maybe a counselor? To the God in us? *Yes*!

I've experienced some things and for a while was confused. I looked at a person professing to be a follower of God as infallible. I was greatly disappointed because of the high esteem given to people who held title within the church. But some of those same people showed hatred, malice, and trickery. I had to realize that they too are just ordinary human beings like me, which makes them fallible. At a point, I held the expectation of expecting the unexpected whenever I stepped through the doors of a church. I don't mean that in a good way. I remember in the last message I heard before moving out of my parents' home, a clergy member said from the pulpit, "If your kids don't want to come to church, kick them out of the house." Hmm, it stuck with me. Yes, I forgave. But we remember certain things because they make such a lasting imprint on our minds.

I moved out of my parents' home at the age of nineteen on a day I stayed home from church, using homework as an excuse. In reality, this was the truth as I purposely waited to complete it so it would clash with the church schedule. At the time, the leader of the church was enforcing the attendance of all children staying with church members. That was the final push that led to my decision to pack my bags and leave.

Before leaving, I left my mother a letter letting her know where I would be, among other things. I remember just a little of what I wrote but not too much. It was a very difficult decision for me as I knew I was leaving my only little sister by herself. But staying would have been too stressful.

I moved into my oldest sister's house, hurt, and confused but ready. As I grew older, I started to develop a relationship with God outside of the church. I have always tried to maintain some type of connection regardless of how I felt about certain circumstances or individuals.

CHAPTER 20:

Access Point

Y access point was and still is Jesus Christ. I started to listen for and see for myself. God and I developed a unique relationship designed to my character. I began to understand God loves me unconditionally, regardless of my past or present. I learned how to transform my mind into a positive structure. Negative thoughts still come, but their tenure is short lived as the positive dominate. I learned how to be grateful and appreciate life even when it seems so unfair. I learned to live one moment at a time. I learned that I was born in America and that plenty of opportunity to achieve exists if I just believe and put forth effort.

Yes, I heard some things in school from many teachers who had positive influences on my life; so for that, I am grateful. But when we truly believe something, it gives us a different drive. I learned that faith is not just waiting but also working for what we desire. I learned that *all* of mankind is fallible, no matter the title, which makes us human beings. I learned to forgive myself as well as others.

I was always taught that God deals with matters of the heart. I didn't fully understand that until when one day, coming home from lunch with a friend, I began to cry and cry and cry from my heart. I had no clue why I was crying, because to me it came from nowhere. But as I cried, I felt something lift from my heart, as if someone came and relieved me of a very heavy load that I was unaware of carrying. Afterwards, I felt exuberantly full of energy. At that moment, I understood the meaning of God dealing with matters of the heart. I now understand how to communicate matters of the heart with God. As my heart speaks, my tongue is silent. I may not always understand what it is saying, but eventually my tongue speaks.

I learned what self-love truly is and how the most powerful love is the love of God. I learned that sometimes bad things happen to good people for what seems to be no apparent reason. I learned that good things happen to people who we may feel do not deserve them. I learned what genuine happiness is and that its origin comes from the heart. I learned what it feels like for my soul to be repaired. I learned that a girl from the inner city can grow to become an author. ☺

I learned that we have to stop blaming everything on divine intervention or its counterpart. There is an in between: *us*. We should account for our mistakes. We often make bad decisions and blame others, but we're the first persons to evaluate so we should adjust accordingly. We repeat too many cycles due to us waiting on divine intervention to fix certain things. Well, sometimes divine intervention is awaiting our arrival. We have attributes we have to unlock. Being able to see, speak, hear, smell, touch, and so on are gifts some of us are privileged enough to possess but often take for granted. How we put these valuables to use is our choice.

I've learned that even when people aren't, God is kind enough to forgive our mistakes. I don't have all of the answers to all of the hurts, but I do know that if we allow, time will heal. It is not always easy for us as individuals, but the load can be shared if we learn to trust God and ourselves. I've learned drinking a glass of wine doesn't commit me to hell. I've learned that I will always make mistakes but that learning from them is most important. I've learned that each person's journey is unique in nature and no two people have the *exact* same spiritual path. We will each experience different detours that are unique.

I've learned to not consider atheists bad people just because they do not believe in God. We never know why a person may not believe in God or understand what they've been through personally. That's their choice. If they are not forcing their beliefs on us or vice versa and are respecting us as human beings, we should be able to get along. I've learned to not judge a book by the cover but to open it up and read it before drawing a conclusion. Going to a building called a church doesn't make it one. The heart of the people who lead the church is what makes it valued as such.

CHAPTER 21:

Fading Away

O NE of my most memorable experiences with God came when stress completely took over my mind, body, and spirit to the point it seemed unbearable. I was unable to correctly function. My strength was very limited. My thoughts ran in circles. I suffered from loss of appetite. I was unable to sleep for weeks. I was unable to think swiftly and quickly to the point I struggled with basic skills like matching socks when putting away the laundry. I suffered from low self-esteem, so I was more susceptible to being lead and manipulated in the wrong direction. I was deeply depressed.

For a while, I fought each day to move my body out of bed because it was so draining to do so. I had just enough energy to make it back and forth to work. Somehow, I kept pushing. One day I said I won't complain and prayed to God in the name of *Jesus*. God, not man, convicted my heart; and I said to God I wouldn't continue to live in my weak state of mind or bad physical condition. I figured it would be better for me to be removed from this earth. I was seeking relief.

One day at work during lunch, one of my friends and I were talking on the phone. In mid-sentence she said, "Oh, my goodness! What is that I'm feeling?" For a while, I had felt I was carrying everything alone and had asked why no one could feel what I was feeling. It was such a struggle I thought anyone who came in connection with me would be able to feel that I was struggling internally. Finally, someone else felt it. She described word for word the feeling and weakness she felt as she spoke to me on the phone. I told her thank you, because now someone knew and understood. She was in shock and was full of deep compassion. I know many people have been through worse, but I thank God for better.

The same friend one night asked if it was difficult for me to fall asleep and if in the process, it felt as if I were dying or fading away. It wasn't a comfortable feeling at all. At that point, I hadn't slept for weeks. That night, she prayed for me and I was finally able to sleep. Man, what a wonderful feeling! My friend was able to connect with me and feel what I was feeling as well as talk to God on my behalf.

Not long after that night, I called my father, who prayed for me over the phone. After he finished praying for me, I felt like my old self for just a few minutes. I was grateful for just feeling like myself again for a moment in time. Yes, the same father who I sometimes view as an overly religious individual prayed for me. There are both a spiritual and a natural side to a person. When a person taps into the spirit of God, the human is no longer in control. I recognize my father is a man who truly loves God and his main goal in life is to please God. Both times of relief gave me hope to keep trying to bounce back.

I went to the doctors to see what was going on. According to their evaluation, everything looked excellent. That was because the battle was spiritual in nature. My soul was in deep repair.

During this ordeal, I remember going to church three times over a two-year span. Each time, I received a special message from God letting me know I should keep moving forward because light was at the end of the tunnel. I believe there is *one God* and *one spirit*, which is why individuals who are in tune can communicate in spiritual harmony. We can make anything or anyone our God, but I believe there to be *one* and *only one* supreme being. ☺

CHAPTER 22:

The Come Back

I STARTED to gradually come back when I was led to open a book I had possessed for years but hadn't read. The book was on self-affirmations. I noticed when I started to read the words that my mind, which was full of negative thoughts, felt relief. For a while, I made it my business to read and say the words every day. I started to increase my intake of water to cleanse my body of toxins. I changed my diet to better suit my unique needs and took up cardio kickboxing. I was learning more of myself. Aristotle, the Greek philosopher and scientist, stated, "Knowing yourself is the beginning of all wisdom." God was guiding my recovery from the inside out. I knew after my recovery I would be better and stronger. Traveling and being more outgoing was becoming a more natural part of my life. I started to increase my knowledge by reading different books, including inspirational scriptures from the Bible researched via Google. I fasted as much as my weak body would allow. My self-esteem and self-respect increased.

The journey was becoming fun as I started to learn the characteristics of God and of myself. See, most people are taught to fear

God, which I certainly do; but that should not be the focal point in our relationship with God. I started to talk to God just as I would to another human being.

One day while at work, a co-worker of mine asked, "Do you fear God?" I replied, "Yes." He then looked at me and said, "He doesn't want you to fear him but to respect him." That was food for thought. I understand to a degree to fear the possible wrath of God; but daily, living life in fear because we may sin against God is no way to live. We are human so we will never be without mistakes. We should try our best to move positively should we choose. Furthermore, just because someone tells us a particular act is a sin doesn't mean it is so. That is between us, God, and perhaps the law.

Getting to know myself was helping me to better relate to others. I sometimes read different sections of the Bible, but the communication from God also started to come from different avenues that better grabbed my attention: nature, autobiographies, music, movies, individuals, and so on. The main thing was to recognize such communication. I'm not speaking of superstition but of genuine communication.

Sometimes we suffer from "analysis paralysis," overanalyzing things to the point it halts progress. To the contrary, however, sometimes we do not look well enough into a situation and are left with the consequences of such impulsive behavior. We should find the balance between the two.

We all have many sides, but sometimes we focus on just one or two, such as our professional side or our religious side. What happens with the many other sides we neglect? When one is operating in the spirit of God, one is not in control. However, when the spirit is not in operation, the self is back in the driver's seat. We as human beings must work on self. There is oneness with God and oneness with self. God helps with both, but we also have to help ourselves.

As humans, we come with many different sides which can be difficult to balance. To name just a few, we have physical, psychological, mental, spiritual, personal, and emotional sides. It is important for us to work on all.

I've learned from experience and by reading *Emotional Intelligence* written by Daniel Goleman that as humans, our initial response to a particular situation tends to come first from the emotional side. According to my readings, this response dates to our ancestry in the way our brains developed to first react emotionally. During those times, survival of the fittest ruled. It was important to have a keen sense of emotions. The lack thereof meant one could be killed more easily. Today, because of our evolvement, we can think more logically and are encouraged to do so rather than to react so quickly based on our emotions. However, it looks like we have a bit more of a journey before this becomes our first or natural reaction. Moreover, the more strongly we personally feel emotionally about a topic, the more aggressively we may pursue that subject. For example, if a clergy member believes homosexuality is wrong because of religious beliefs and has a personal dislike for homosexuality, those personal feelings may spark emotions which cause that clergy member to make it a point of emphasis to express that displeasure during a sermon where a known homosexual is in attendance.

If the personal emotion is controlled, perhaps a more logical message of love can overshadow emotions of ill will. Delivery of what one believes is primary. However, letting personal thoughts completely take over and not allowing God to speak through and during a sermon is immature. Targeting an individual or a group of individuals with opposing views is a bit self-righteous. We never know the reason for someone going to church on a given day. That may be that person's last chance to acquire help.

One more example where *other* emotions may overpower love is when a clergy member who may be a survivor of an alcoholically abusive relationship sees a known alcoholic in church attendance and then emphasizes during the sermon a personal displeasure with alcoholism. Again, perhaps a message of love can overshadow personal views and emotions about a particular subject. It's not an easy task but definitely achievable.

Many have overcome major life setbacks but never stepped into a church to do so. Some were able to tap into their inner beings, exercising will power and determination as well as belief in themselves to achieve what seemed impossible. They unlocked certain things possessed by their higher inner beings. Others needed an act of God to unleash their supernatural because self was not enough to overcome.

I personally know a few recovering alcoholics who overcame by successfully completing an AA program. Then there are ones who went cold turkey, even after years of alcohol abuse. As mentioned before, I've also witnessed the overcoming of alcohol abuse through an act of God. I also know a few individuals for whom, unfortunately, the AA program was not as successful as hoped and some who, after submission to divine intervention, returned to alcohol abuse. My point is that when one route doesn't work, perhaps we can try another; and if that route doesn't work, we should keep trying, one way or another. We should find the root of the issue and then properly attack it.

We can find counsel both inside and outside of the church. Sometimes, it works one way; other times, it works the other way. The objective is to find what works for us as individuals. Ultimately, it is our choice. If we genuinely want freedom from something, we will be guided in the right direction. The important thing is to not make excuses along our path. We may have to overcome and subdue hereditary as well as environmental conditions, which may be very difficult at times but not impossible. We can try it on our own; but from my personal experiences, it is easier with God's assistance. Adapting to change is human nature.

Hopefully, we all understand that some problems are just too tough for us to solely resolve with the abilities we possess and that we need a little more help from God. At times, we may also need help from family members, friends, significant others, clergy members, social workers, and so on. All things considered, showing gratitude for the help should be sufficient. I try to acknowledge not only the source for providing the help but also God for sending the help.

However, sometimes help comes in the disguise of individuals who have ulterior motives. Wisdom will help us to determine the genuine nature of help. I believe all wisdom comes from God through life experiences. Learn to live a little. ☺

As a culture, we are used to seeing and hearing certain things from people who believe in and trust God. Well, an upcoming generation is shaking up things and expanding minds that once were trapped into boxed thinking: Minds that are wiser and open to miracles not yet seen in this present time. Minds who ask questions like what did people use as a guide to learn God before any Bible was written. Minds who ask questions like how is it that atheists show more love than some believers in God. Is it because they display human characteristics such as love, care, hope, and good conversation without negative, preconceived ideas because we do not believe the same?

I still struggle with plenty of personal things but make it a point to work on them. Many of us experienced things as children, before we were able to control the outcomes, which still affect us today. Some of us may not even remember some of the occurrences, but we can feel that something is wrong, so we desperately seek answers. Other things we remember vividly, things that seem to have torn our very souls apart. Without realizing it, we have this little person following us around, still controlling our lives. We express this in bad habits that we refuse to break, anger that is easy to trigger, pain that lingers, unresolved feelings of not feeling loved or wanted, a shown vulnerability to men or women, a promiscuous nature, untruthfulness that has become habitual, low self-esteem, and the list goes on and on. These are human-based issues that need to be addressed head on with time and understanding.

CHAPTER 23:

Understanding Self

H AVE you ever witnessed persons who are quick to anger respond in this way when you mention it to them: *"I'm not angry!"* Even within their responses, their eyes are popped, their hearts are rapidly beating, and they are very defensive. One of the definitions of anger is a strong feeling of annoyance, displeasure, or hostility. You be the judge.

Anger is a human characteristic that can be used in a very positive way. Anger can cause positive change. However, I'm not speaking of that kind of anger. I'm speaking of the type of anger that is easily provoked and causes negative chain reactions.

The first thing we should do is admit to ourselves that we have certain issues, even if it reveals our weaknesses and vulnerabilities. Lying to ourselves is an awful thing to do. If we are not honest with ourselves, how can we honestly expect to progress? Once we are able to be truthful with ourselves, we can more readily accept corrective action. If we are not honest with our own being, we should not expect to be completely honest with anyone else. Sometimes we may not be aware of our flawed behavior; but I hope reasonably minded people exist within our circle of family or friends who can always provide good sound advice that has and will continue to prove beneficial to our development.

A constant struggle exists between our natural and spiritual characteristics. We are still evolving as humans and have so much more to learn of ourselves. Science helps us to ascertain the many attributes we possess and how they operate. The goal is to stop shortchanging what we possess as unique creatures. All sides to our unique design help us to understand how truly special we are.

I believe in the science behind our human development. Can God and science not co-exist? I believe that God created science. For example, the brain consists of three main parts: the cerebrum, the cerebellum, and the brain stem.[1] The cerebrum possesses the frontal lobe, parietal lobe, sensory cortex, motor cortex, temporal lobe, Wernicke's area, occipital lobe, and Broca's area. The cerebellum contains the limbic system, the amygdala, the hippocampus, the hypothalamus, and the thalamus. The brain stem contains the midbrain, pons, and medulla.

For those who may not be able to pronounce some of these words, no worries. I had to use YouTube to learn how to pronounce *amygdala*. The point of my listing the many portions of the brain is not to bore you with science but to show how science has uncovered these diverse portions of the brain and is continuing to develop an understanding of their functionalities. I believe God provides the understanding in the science of human creation. I personally do not believe the other way around, that science created human beings. But to each

---

[1] From "Parts of the Brain and Their Functions," *MDHealth.com*, accessed 12/5/2020, http://www.md-health.com/Parts-Of-The-Brain-And-Function.

his own. Are there scientists who believe in God? I believe there are plenty. Are there scientists who do not believe in God? I believe there are plenty. Again, to each his own.

Understanding how we are, maybe not even on a scientific level but from previous experiences, will help us to better understand our usual behavior in diverse settings. The learning should help prevent us from putting ourselves in subsequent unfavorable situations similar in nature.

Knowing God should also help us to better understand how truly special we are, regardless of any unfavorable circumstances life may predetermine.

I mentioned that I work on positive affirmations daily, which has truly helped to reshape my thought process. I advise you to do the same, even if it just involves you writing personal affirmations and goals down and then remembering to recite them every day. From what I've learned, all positive affirmations have to first start with "I am" or "I have." For example, "I am very strong, and I am getting stronger." Design the affirmations specific to you and what you believe to possess in character. The important thing is to say them with meaning. An abundance of positive affirmations can also be found on the Internet.

Each day the affirmations may change according to what objective one is trying to accomplish, which is great because diversity expands one's horizon. After a while, the positive thoughts will dominate the negative. Because it is a process that takes time, patience is required for such life-time transitions. It can be tedious at times, but force feeding an affirmation is not advised. Asking effective questions will further help the cause.

One more note I will mention is that listening to positive affirmations on a daily basis also helps to retune our thought processes. I've personally experienced this method, which is termed auto suggestion.

Sometimes we place too much emphasis on religion or spirituality, which creates an imbalance between our natural character and our spiritual character. While in spiritual bliss, we feel supernatural, as if we are the only ones interconnected with our higher power. The feeling is *ah-h-h-h-ma-a-a-zing*, one we do not wish to relinquish. When we come down from our high, we slowly transcend into our "human" character. Slowly but surely, we start to feel those emotions that we feel as humans: drained, sad, depressed, frustrated, hurt, happy, calm, excited, joyous, and so on.

As negative emotions develop, we should try saying the reverse of what we are feeling instead of giving in to the negativity. For example, when feeling sad, say with meaning, "I am okay" or "I am genuinely happy." I am not suggesting avoiding responsibly expressing disparaging human emotions at times. It is imperative for us to do so such as in the natural grieving process. Otherwise, we tend to try to behave perfectly or to be too concerned with the opinion of others. Some days are better than others, which may reflect in our demeanor. But we should also learn how to soothe ourselves.

I do a lot of positive inner self-talk to build mental strength. In this positive talk, I try to be realistic as well. In our positive thoughts, we should start to make positive movements. Often, things are not within our control; but we tend not to control those things we are able to control in a productive manner. I am also a strong believer in the wisdom of being a silent learner. In other words, most of the time, we need say nothing, just learn and observe.

I'm all for positive talk, but do not let people use this to their advantage. Some may mistake kindness as a weakness. Sometimes when speaking to others, we should deliver our message as thoroughly and positively aggressively as possible. Other times we have to be a little hard-hearted because other methods of communication have failed. For example, when we must constantly tell our significant others to remove their shoes from the middle of the floor, we may deliver the first few requests politely. But each time we have to repeat the request, our voices become a little more edgy and eventually possibly result in us doing something to teach a lesson that will ensure the same issue is not repeated.

CHAPTER 24:

Calm Comes after the Storm

THE church is supposed to be for those who are seeking help. If someone goes for help but hears only ridicule for being a "sinner," is the mission of the church/nonprofit organization being fulfilled? The church should be in position to deliver nonjudgmental acts or gestures that help to restore.

Churches fulfilling their genuine purpose are sometimes abused and overused. There are plenty of con artists who will walk into churches appearing to do and mean well, but the entire time they are just looking to use good-hearted individuals for materialistic gain. Everyone, including clergy members, has a limit; and no one should tolerate being used. Expecting people to withstand certain heinous acts because of their titles within the church is just a way to try to use their love of God or of people against them. Even God gets angry at times.

Society has developed a dependency on the one or two stronger persons within a particular group or family who carry the weight of the entire pack. In turn, the stronger ones become drained from over support. Just because some are viewed as stronger individuals doesn't mean they should take on or try to solve everyone else's problems. Being out of position in someone's life will cause us to expend energy on purposeless ventures. This leaves us with a regretful feeling after helping someone out of similar situations numerous times. There is love and there is pity. I'm still learning to balance the two. Constantly feeling sorry for certain people will leave us with empty wallets and broken hearts.

Have you ever intended to break up with someone but when you begin to do so, the person starts a sob story? As a result, you feel sorry for that person and ultimately stay against your desires. This is a game. There is nothing much worse than constantly pitying an individual. The default is that we become enablers.

We should help each other become better but not continually provide a buffer to individuals. When we do that, we hold people back from finding and fulfilling their purpose in life. Why find a purpose when they have a crutch to use as an escape when something happens? Dare to be strong and say, "I refuse to be your door mat any longer." Then dare that person who has been dependent for so long to find his or her better self.

We can then use the energy we are expending to help those who are just using us to help those who are truly in need of help such as the less fortunate who are homeless or who are battling terminal diseases or perhaps, again, just ourselves. Some of the money being used to keep the clergy in their expensive cars can be donated to reputable nonprofits should someone in the household not need it for a worthy cause. As mentioned before, I do believe charity begins at home.

Why do some say love but show hate? I believe it is because they have some personal issues with self that need to be addressed. Before

I went through a deep spiritual cleanse, I could not feel other people; nor did I care to possess this ability. Without realizing it, I hurt many people. Then, again, some I intentionally and maliciously hurt out of revenge. I'm no saint, but I've tried to adjust certain behavior and have unlocked some of my ability to relate to others and show compassion. It is up to us to learn the rules of life one way or another. To this point, I believe my most memorable Ruby and God experience unlocked some personal attributes. On my journey back, I learned a lot about myself; and I am sure I will forever be learning. To sum it up, I had to look within myself to find God. ☺

Peace of mind is so precious. I didn't realize how precious until my peace of mind was taken. I mentioned earlier that my mind was circling at a tremendously rapid pace. I've heard of people constantly thinking, which I still tend to do from time to time; but I'm speaking of rapid racing in circles to where you are not in control of your thoughts and certain thoughts continually cycle. What an experience! The ability to make wise decisions is a little obscured because everything seems to be viewed through blurred vision.

How did I regain peace? I started with prayer, of course. After-wards, I listened to what my prayers provoked. Naturally, I listened to music, which always soothes me; but I needed more. I read in the book of affirmations previously mentioned that a mantra, which is defined as a word or sound repeated to aid concentration in meditation, is a good way to ease the mind. The book then took it a step further by suggesting one meditates at least thirty minutes daily. Before that point in my life, I really didn't care to meditate; but I was desperate. The advice in the book suggested concentrating on a positive affirmation would suffice or just a soft melody that eases the mind.

It took me about fifteen minutes, give or take, to really zone in on an affirmation such as "I am at peace with myself." Other times I listened to soft melodies, not songs, to clear my mind. This also took about the same amount of time for my mind to settle; but once I got there, oh, my, what an awesome relief!

I am a strong believer in the power of prayer. Growing up, I remember being taught meditation on the word of God. However, I was not introduced to meditation on other things, such as positive affirmations or just oneness, until more recently. All are effective, but the purpose being sought before the meditation session begins should determine its focal point. Although I do not focus on people or things, at times I do focus on one name: Jesus. I also ensure that the room is quiet and lightly lit. There are experts who can help with the meditation process, so if interested, conduct some personal research to explore the topic. Note: The book, *The Meditative Mind* by Daniel Goleman, is a great resource.

CHAPTER 25:

Move Something besides Lips

H AVE you ever explained an issue to someone and received this response: "Just pray about it"? Well, sometimes we just simply need to take positively aggressive action. The phrase "just pray about it" is sometimes used as an excuse to sit back and be lazy. Jesus mastered *faith*. We may pray for some things that are beyond our control; but other times, we use prayer as an excuse to bury issues without thorough examination. Every situation encountered is not a cause for prayer. Sometimes a personal kick in the butt is in order. There is a great distinction between *fantasy* and *faith*.

We can also take steps before we pray on certain issues that are initially within our control, such as securing car insurance or roadside assistance before something happens to a vehicle. Any person's financial or life status can change due to extenuating circumstances that may prevent one from being able to make a payment, so there are some exceptions. This is just a general example.

Praying for the same thing over and over without working towards the request is not something that will produce better results. At a point, we are just beating air. Everything for which we pray will not come to focus. Sometimes God hears our prayers and answers a painful *no* we have to accept. For instance, we may ask for our loved one's life to be spared but God takes them away. The God who most of us believe took the loved one away is the same God we pray to in requesting strength to help us through the natural grieving process without holding resentment. Sometimes the no to certain requests is to protect us. Sometimes we do not understand and perhaps never will, but the best we can do is accept.

We also have to be careful not to pray for vain things, such as "God please make me rich." There are riches all over the United States of America, so we should go after them as productively as possible. Besides, if some of us were granted the request of becoming rich, we would probably forget God as soon as the money changed hands.

Only praying to God when there is an issue but neglecting to do so when things are going fine is not the best relationship to develop. It makes it seem we are taking for granted the things we are blessed with, which we all may do at times, such as waking up, having a job, or being able to see and hear.

Have you ever experienced persons who only called when they need money or help with a problem? In the case of borrowing money, once the money changed hands, the borrower disappeared. When you finally caught up with them and asked for repayment, did these borrowers display an attitude? If so, how did it make you feel? Used, upset, hurt, or angry? Wouldn't hearing from these persons when nothing was needed be nice? Perhaps if they initiated contact for an exchange of conversation that focused on well-being for both of you when things were going well for them, they would create better balance instead of one-sided beneficiary relationships.

The same goes for other relationships. If one person in the relationship is constantly providing but is not reciprocated to some degree, it will create an imbalance because of one constantly feeling neglected. If the imbalance continues, the relationship will eventually self-destruct. In summary, acknowledging God regardless of what is going on in life will help create a better relationship.

Letting someone know what they need to do and showing them how to do it are two different responsibilities. Telling me that I need to have faith is one thing, but showing me how to use faith is another, just as saying you have a good voice is different from showing you have a good voice. To me, the best example of perfecting faith was Jesus. However, some choose to follow a different exemplified leader, which is their choice. Is there more than one way to the same God? ☺

CHAPTER 26:

Life Rules

FROM my observations, I've learned some life rules. I believe in karma because of my life experiences. At times, God's mercy, as well as the mercy of individuals, released me from the grip of karma. We do not receive everything deserved; otherwise, I certainly would be in a pitiful state, if not nonexistent. The decisions I made greatly impacted outcomes. Becoming better at decision making is something I try to continue to work on. We sometimes place too much responsibility on God or other people. We first have to become better in our decision making and take ownership of our mistakes.

I try to be cautious in the way I treat others. But I always remember to be tolerant within reason, not allowing someone to take advantage of my kindness. Some of our insecurities come from unknown places. For example, whenever we have someone in authority who overuses power, that person is more than likely substituting to compensate for whatever the person may lack. The only way such individuals build their self-esteem is to constantly strip others of theirs. We should not allow anyone to take our self-esteem. Naturally, our confidence may be a little shaken at times; but that can be rebuilt with a little effort.

Take, for example, bosses who seem to like coming into work to constantly flex their muscles, so everyone is reminded of who is in charge. It could be that these individuals do not get the opportunity to be the boss at home; so when they get to work, they abuse power. To sum it up, they go home and have their self-esteem stripped then return to work to rebuild it by stripping others of theirs.

The same goes for human beings who cannot be faithful or loyal to their significant others who deserve such. The issue is not about the loyal persons; it is the disloyal persons who have internal issues to resolve. These can come from not being able to trust that they are worthy of such loyalty and so, at the expense of hurting people, continually betray. On the other hand, the disloyal provide better treatment to those who treat them in the way they truly see themselves, which is unworthy. The issues could also stem from experiencing the betrayal of those to whom they were once loyal. In moving forward, these individuals' natural inclination is to distrust future encounters; so being disloyal comes quite easily. Although this may be a reason, it is certainly not an excuse.

Some of the most loyal people have been hurt by the very ones to whom they showed unwavering loyalty because someone new entered the picture. Although the new person might have not earned loyalty, that new thrilling feeling comingled with superficial selfish desires overshadowed any loyalty received from the impacted family member, friend, or significant other. Not too many people understand the value of true loyalty in family, business, relationships, or friendships, as most of the time it is exchanged for a penis, a vagina, biased religious beliefs, or money.

As far as those who are loyal, do not provide loyalty to someone undeserving. Move on to someone who does, even if that means transferring that loyalty to self. I believe the most valuable loyalties are to God and self.

When we put someone ahead of everyone, including ourselves, we create an opportunity for the beneficiary to take for granted any unearned good deed provided. I've experienced being overly responsible for other people's issues. I'm learning to handle only my business, not being selfish but learning to balance when to help and when to back off. We often spend much time trying to solve the issues of other people who are very capable of personally resolving them. When do we make time to solve our own personal issues and really evaluate our personal needs?

Do not make life too easy for anyone because the person's preset will be an expectation for certain things, even if unearned. A little resistance will go a long way in building character.

Some of us who behave foolishly are sometimes not as foolish as we may appear. Sometimes we behave selfishly, not caring how certain behavior can negatively impact others. For example, when our significant others take bill money to pay for new shoes without our knowledge, we may make a statement like this: "Why would you do something so dumb"? The first thing we tend to think is that these persons lack some mental capacity to calculate the ripple effect of certain behavior. But that is not always the case. Sometimes these individuals have already calculated the negative impact but do not care enough to deter from committing the act. The result is an "oh, well" mentality.

Sometimes when we have done wrong, we try to put it on everyone else but ourselves. In fact, some people will make excuses on behalf of repeated wrongdoers as if they are representing them in a court of law. Regardless of the nature and the reason we do something, we should own our wrongs, especially as adults. Children go back and forth in blaming each other for offenses. Adults should mature mentally, as well as chronologically, to distinguish between the two approaches.

For example, when we are inexcusably late for an important event, we may make every excuse in the book instead of just admitting we are wrong, and that better planning would have prevented such an outcome. It sounds simple, but we sometimes make it difficult. After admitting the wrong, to show we truly mean what we say, we should avoid repeating the act as best as possible. Eventually, with practice, we will eliminate it. As the saying goes, old habits die hard; so some things may take a little more time to correct than others. Even after correction, we may slip up every now and again.

It is not so much about how much we earn or make but what we do with what we earn or make. I believe we all would love to make more money and, if we had the choice between a six-figure salary and a five-figure salary, would more than likely choose the six-figure salary. But productivity should not stop for us after earning or making money.

I've witnessed a person who earned a six-figure salary struggle, while a person with a similar family status and personal obligations who earned a lower-middle class income lived a rather comfortable life. I guess dollars make cents but not sense.

It is very important that we ask ourselves effective questions that will produce reasonable answers. Personally, asking myself certain questions when my mind seems trapped helps me to come to better, reasonable conclusions. For example, asking myself why I was always late for events helped me to conclude that I needed to become better at time management and preparing the days before the event. Seems simple, but I was not as dependable until I asked myself that question. There are very few excuses for showing up unreasonably late or missing important events of loved ones.

Our hearts are very delicate vessels. Sometimes we think too much with our hearts and less with our brains. If we learn to exercise more brain power, we will implement logic more easily into our daily life choices, minimizing emotional decisions that may not be as beneficial. Allowing ourselves time for emotions to subside and logic to prevail will train our minds to become stronger in effective problem solving.

A major factor that may weigh in on the progress of a friendship or family life is how well we balance our significant others with them. Every relationship comes with limits. If people are unable to fairly balance loved ones and friends because everything has to always be about their relationships or lackluster love life, including during girls' or guys' nights out, phone conversations, vacations, work, church, and so on, they should put more effort into discussing a variety of topics that are not self-centered.

It is very important to discuss personal relationships with loved ones. However, it becomes overwhelming when we make it a continual priority to overshadow other topics that may be of importance to our loved ones. Because of selfish objectives and closed mindedness, we may find we are in the same repetitive predicament for which the relationship or lackluster love life is responsible.

The inability of people to take personal time with close friends or family members because of insecurity within relationships or gullibility for their significant others greatly impacts the dynamic of those relationships. To some degree, we are all about our significant others, which is fine. But family and friends offer things of value that signifi-cant others may not and vice versa.

We can treat all parties honorably. It is not fair to family or friends to only hear from us when something in a relationship goes to the left. This also goes for individuals who continually put family before their relationships. We can accomplish better balance with a little more observation and effort.

If we observe closely, we may find that, if we are treating some people incorrectly, the very ones we least want to hurt us will do so because it is a round world. It will hurt to the core. Life is unfair at times, and we cannot explain some things. Some acts are egregious, and no one deserves them as a human being, but other things are simply justified.

Never settle for less than what we know we deserve, which is nothing but the best. Being able to provide this for self helps eliminate acceptance of subpar behavior from others. I've learned that trying to control others will leave one in a vulnerable and angry position because there will be constant micromanaging of an imaginary power. We cannot fully control the actions of others, nor should we try to control capable adults. Those who lack self-control often try to control others.

When we are ready, life will present certain opportunities, but not before then. For example, sometimes before we elevate finan-cially, we will have to remove certain individuals from our intimate circle. If not, money may go to unproductive causes such as unworthy boyfriends, girlfriends, family members, investors, or friends, who will blow through the money then return in demand of more. The soft hearts we may have for individuals may overwhelm our logic so that we see giving as a way of loving or perhaps of keeping these individuals. After a while, the money vanishes; and, soon after, so go these charity cases.

We should be as realistic as possible in setting goals. Being optimistic and hopeful is something we should all work towards; but in that optimism, it is important to establish how our current situation may impact our outcome. For example, if we set a goal to save a certain dollar amount within a specific time but continue with unresolved poor spending habits, the optimism and hope of saving that money is just as imaginative as the mind of an author writing nonfiction.

We not only have to think big but also move big. Reviewing the facts and remaining optimistic as we progress to move some of the opposition in view of our goals will create a more realistic approach to our big thinking and ultimately produce possibly bigger results. It all starts with our mentality. I believe the mind controls the body but, hopefully, soon after will come movement.

When something good happens, we should not look for something bad to follow. Expecting good things but being prepared for the worst is a good mentality to acquire. Sometimes it is very difficult to think positively on a daily basis; but with more of an inner push, it is accomplishable. We tend to always think the worst will happen even when something good happens to us. Accepting good and expecting better to come provides better peace of mind.

We should not put anything past anyone because we sometimes surprise ourselves with uncharacteristic behavior. Surely, then, we can expect this to be the case for other human beings. We trust some people to not behave in a particular manner; so, when we find that one of those persons has behaved uncharacteristically, before concluding concerning that behavior, it is important for us to first evaluate ourselves.

Uncomfortable positions can turn out to be very rewarding. For example, we may wear something unpredictable yet fashionable or do something unexpected that breaks routine.

Sometimes, giving and expecting nothing in return ensures that when help is not reciprocated, we are not left with regretful feelings.

It is okay to ask a favor, but it is also okay to expect one in return. Sometimes help comes in the least expected form, so we should learn to accept.

Friends are truly an invaluable piece of life. If we have at least one good friend, we should cherish that person because *true* friendship is a rarity nowadays.

Saying no to some things will spare a lot of people from dipping and dodging when it is time for them to fulfill the request. Being able to give back is a blessing, so we should try to do so often, but not at the expense of deprived living.

Knowing who we are eliminates someone else from defining us. Getting to know self is one of the best things I ever did and continue to do. Getting to know self will help you to better understand others. I do not know everything about myself, but I try to observe my characteristics very carefully. Some may call this being self-conscious. The reason is that there is always someone watching us, even when we do not realize it. If someone can learn us from the inside out but we are unaware of our behavior, their awareness can be used either for or against us. We should not allow anyone to know us to the point they are able to become our masters due to us surrendering as their puppets.

Having influential people to help our better character develop due to their ability to see and bring out the best in us is an invaluable blessing that one should behold. The acceptance of that help will prove tremendously beneficial. Their vantage point and insight can reveal what is not already personally known. At times, the hardest person to see is self; so a little help along the way is a good thing.

Why are we so inclined to accept something negative that someone speaks of us but when someone speaks positively of us, we are not as receptive? Is it because as humans our natural inclination is to think negatively of ourselves? Being modest is awesome but thinking low of self is detrimental to the cycle of life.

Being adventurous and trying something new opens the mind. Excitement provides a temporary adrenaline rush, but it does not define true happiness. Happiness comes from within. Even without excitement, it fully satisfies.

We should not try too hard to understand unreasonable behavior. When people behave unreasonably, the tendency is to try to understand the unreasonableness. But, in doing so, we lower our mentality. Instead of trying to understand what we view as unreasonable behavior, we should try to help the perpetrators understand reasonable thinking, should they choose to embrace it. For example, when a child misbehaves, the parent may try to explain reasonable behavior to the child to prevent repeated offenses. In doing so, the parent does not adopt the mentality of the child because it is conclusive the behavior is unreasonable. Instead, the parent may ask of the child why he or she displayed certain behavior to better understand the child's thought processes. Then the child can reinvent a way of thinking approved at the advice of the parent.

Listening is so much better than talking because so much more is learned. This is hard to perfect, but I'm told I've gotten better. ☺ I'll get there. The main thing is that I'm willing to work on being better. It is very hard to do because some topics are so intriguing or personal in nature that just a minute of waiting to respond seems like eternity.

Sometimes the thing that keeps me from responding is the ability to control compulsion. That is basically what it narrows to. Compulsive behavior makes us want to immediately gratify a craving. Self-control keeps this in order. We can employ different brain games to help decrease compulsive behavior; however, nothing is better than real life practice.

Trying to change someone who rejects it leaves the aggressor feeling drained due to resistance to the change. We have to accept people for who they are. It is very energy consuming trying to change someone who does not desire to do so. We sometimes expect the best out of people, but the truth is most people rarely show their best because they choose not to do so. Then, there are times when someone's best is simply not enough.

We cannot fully control the acts of others. However, we can control acts of our own. Over willing ourselves to fulfill other people's dreams that they simply do not desire to fulfill is selfish not of these persons but of us because we are trying to control the acts of others. If they choose not to be the best or who we perceive them to be, that is their personal choice. It is also our personal choice to move on by fulfilling the personal dreams we set for ourselves.

Being open-minded leads to more opportunity than being close-minded, which may overlook opportunity. I was once trapped into one-way thinking and was not open to all possibilities. My upbringing had a lot to do with this mentality. For instance, because growing up I learned the behavior of not accepting any opposing views when it came to certain things, I adopted this practice concerning opinions or ideas of my own. My mind was one sided; so sometimes when people mentioned something that was in opposition to my thoughts, I didn't even consider they may have been correct. When I adopted flexibility with my thought processes, I was able to better relate to people. I may not have always adopted their thoughts, but I at least learned to keep an open mind and consider them.

I am concrete on some things and will not bend, such as my belief in God. But generally, I try to keep an open mind to everyday life experiences because enlightenment can come at any moment. No one knows everything. Those who may seem to know it all can be intrusive. Sometimes allowing a person to learn by experience is the best route.

Sometimes the best advice to follow is our own. So many of us can give out some pretty good advice; but when it comes to us following that same good advice, we do the exact opposite. Hmm.

Criticism is mostly seen as a negative thing. But people who love us need to sometimes criticize our behavior constructively because it may be difficult for us to see. Someone who loves us will be honest, even when it hurts. When people who love us tell us truths that may hurt, we may say, "Don't judge me." But their judgment of character, their constructive criticism, is based on facts.

I know I have had some of my best friends provide the best judgment calls on certain acts or spoken thoughts. Actually, they warned me of some things which, had I listened, I would've better liked the end result. But we live and hopefully learn. The people closest to us should be welcomed with open arms in providing advice, but the advisors must not come off as judgmental. Presentation is everything. On the other hand, we have those who are overly sensitive to any kind of constructive criticism, which makes it harder for loved ones to even offer advice on possible bad decisions.

We may ask and be granted certain requests that are not for us, which usually carries a hefty price, such as asking for a man or woman to come into our lives because we are tired of being alone. How much of ourselves are we willing to sacrifice to gain and keep a significant other? Desperate times usually call for desperate measures. We lower our expectations so greatly to accommodate our request that, as time grows, we become more and more miserable. The price we are paying in receipt of the request is much greater than the reward.

We rationalize this behavior by saying it is better than being alone. Feeling alone is just that, a feeling, which is why even when some of us are in relationships or marriages, we still feel alone. It is important to understand we always have ourselves and, should one choose, God. We should be grateful for that because eventually someone who appreciates us will come along to provide the mutual love we so deserve. How can someone respect or love someone who does not demand that in character? Believe it or not, there are plenty of very happy singles who refuse to settle.

Even some of the most seemingly confident people demonstrate low self-esteem through their behavior. People who continuously need complimenting or validation have low self-esteem complexes. Inner confidence will minimize some of the need to hear validation. Hearing good things from others is great but being dependent on such compliments reveals inner issues. Sometimes people with low self-esteem build theirs by tearing down others, even at the expense of taking possession of another's self-respect or esteem.

Insecurity sometimes plays a big role in infidelity or the player world. In this instance, once a challenge (a man or woman) has been conquered, the thrill is gone. So, to boost ego, the player once again zooms in on a new target. The new man or woman becomes the priority because it boosts the ego or self-esteem of the player to know that someone else wants to be with him or her. Perhaps the challenge rests in wanting someone else who provides a little bit of a chase. Once that mission is accomplished and the thrill is gone, the next target is imminent.

Each conquered challenge boosts the ego, producing an over-whelming dose of arrogance. Without this slew of secondary approval, the security for the self-worth of said individual is in jeopardy. It must be a constant new reminder that says, "Hey, you're great!" Even hearing it from their "main squeeze" does not satisfy because that thrill has long been surpassed.

A self-confident person does not need to validate self by manip-ulating or dogging others. A self-confident person can appreciate the mutual loyalty and trust within a relationship. The encouragement from just that one person means the absolute world, and no other woman or man can have such an impression. Confidence can come from within as well as from another individual.

Dating, which can lead to meeting a lot of people until one finds the right candidate (should that be the objective), cannot only be fun but also exhausting. Dating and being honest are not what I view as behaving as a player. Dating multiple people and being untruthful about it leans more towards that category.

Can you say Olivia Pope? ☺ For those who may not know, Olivia Pope was a character played by actress Kerry Washington in the tele-vision series *Scandal*, written by Shonda Rhimes. In short, she was a character who had an occupation that involved solving other people's problems. Unfortunately, in reality, some people are trying to be Olivia Pope's character. Helping someone in need is an awesome thing. I often receive much help and try to help others when it is possible or not too imposing. However, the neglect of addressing personal issues is a recipe for personal disaster. As the personal neglect occurs, a build-up forms that eventually clashes.

Why is it that we do this to ourselves? Is it because we think we are okay, so we have to get everyone else in position? Is it because facing our problems is too scary or is such a complicated task that we do not want to confront certain issues sensitive to our hearts? Is it because we are completely blind to our own characters? Is it because we do not take the time to provide self-nurturing? Whatever the case, to efficiently help others, we should ensure we first help ourselves so that self-efficiency does not decline. For example, individuals who like to visit homeless shelters to feed the less fortunate but suddenly are unable to do so as often as desired because of their own bad eating habits or of not properly taking care of themselves should explore and execute better health objectives so they can fulfill their desires.

Sometimes letting go is the main hold up for some individuals acquiring success. Letting go of people who mean so much but hurts our chances of success is one of the hardest things for the heart to achieve. But when we accomplish it, time ensures the healing process occurs. These individuals with whom we choose to surround ourselves are detriments to our character. One bad apple can truly spoil the whole bunch. We should throw away the bad apples before they infiltrate the entire bunch.

One of the many joys in life is the experience of true love in a relationship. Conversely, one of the best triumphs is the bounce back after a heart break. I know this sounds contradictory but making the best of a breakup is an experience that helped me build tremendous character. Not allowing the breakup to break me but to help me restructure, increased my self-confidence and awareness of how awesome I truly am.

Rebuilding ourselves after relationships where we seemed to have given our all is difficult to accomplish. Sometimes what makes it most difficult is that to move on, we should let go of trust issues that exist because of the nature of the previous relationship.

Learning to not judge the next person by the previous person's actions and recognizing clear signs of repeated cycles require a complicated balance we must find to be truly happy in a relationship. Moving on too quickly sometimes clouds our better judgment because we have not allowed ourselves time to nurture the heart break. We tend to look for that nurturing in the next candidate of choice.

Waiting forever to move on is also not recommended. Allowing for some time to heal a broken heart helps. One can use the extra energy on more productive things, like taking a cooking lesson, reading a book, writing a book, taking up a hobby, starting a business, or just hanging out with friends and family.

Sometimes the phrase "everything happens for a reason" is misguided. It is often used to cover bad decisions or ill-advised moves. Bad results do occur for a reason, bad relationships do exist for a reason, constantly facing financial hardships due to poor financial planning does happen for a reason, and the list goes on and on. Sometimes, the reason is simply because poor decisions were made prior to the outcome and better planning in the future will produce better results: Daily, I listen to *Born to Be Exceptional,* an affirmations CD by Steve Norris, that states, "Failure is nothing more than a need to modify my approach."

To add, the phrase "I do not live my life in regret" to justify a wrong committed against someone is not the appropriate response to provide when seeking reconciliation. Living life in regret is not something anyone should do. However, considering the feelings of others regardless of what opportunity time presents is more of an adult-like demeanor to exercise. In turn, the possible betrayal that may lead to a narrow-minded response, such as "I do not live my life in regret," to justify a wrong will be eradicated.

Knowing something is usually not enough. Doing something with what we know substantiates that knowledge. For instance, someone who is on a sweets restriction but still chooses to eat that extra donut reveals that knowing about the sweets restriction and its consequences is not enough. Not eating the extra donut because of the awareness would substantiate that knowledge, which, when exercised, is wisdom.

We often treat the ones closest to us less valuably than new encounters. The ones closest to us should be treated with the most delicacy and care. If the intent is for those persons to be around for as long as possible in good health and spirits, why not contribute as much as possible to that cause?

Believing what people show us rather than what they say is a remedy to preventing repetitive destructive cycles. If people constantly say one thing but do another, they are basically lying. Each time they repeat the habit, and we accept because of emotional words makes it easier for them to repeat offenses. Because there is no resistance to motivate alternate correction, unfulfilled words satisfy.

If these behaviors are repeatedly accepted with no further resolve but a bunch of meaningless words being recited to mend broken hearts or disappointment, a wish list for these persons to change becomes priority. Commanding respect in any relationship should be a priority, not just by saying so but by showing certain behavior will not be tolerated. If someone in a relationship refuses to show respect on any level, the relationship should cease. Building inner strength is a must to execute such resilience.

Is respect from someone who allegedly shares a mutual love too much to ask? It should be a given. True love is loyal and trustworthy. Fabricated love feels more like uncertainty coupled with stupidity.

Life has such an amazing sense of humor. I'm sure we can all think of unfavorable situations that brought laughter because of the unbelievable timing. Such instances seemed to unfold at the most inopportune times and would've been more convenient had they happened the first ninety-nine chances around instead of on the one-hundredth.

God too has a sense of humor that continually tests the character and trust of human beings. These tests are often overlooked, so the preset is to repeat cycles without understanding that adjustments need to be made within our character to pass the tests and move to the next level.

It is okay to feel the natural emotion of fear. It is what we do with that fear that determines its impact. Two things can happen: Fear can drive us or paralyze us.

These life rules I've listed were acquired by observing and learning human behavior, including my own. We all have distinct attributes, but we also share a lot of predictable human associations. Every human is unique, but we possess general similarities. Even if separated by certain classes or geographic areas, we can always find someone who shares similar characteristics with another human being, including ourselves.

Previously, I listed many rules regulated by the religion in which I was raised. Sometimes I felt those rules weighed heavily on the freedom we possess in the US of A. However, those rules combined with the life rules learned thus far have certainly served a vital purpose in my development. I do not believe that God blessed me or my family in being born in the United States of America to be so limited in thinking or movement. Even God gives us freedom to choose.

CHAPTER 27:

Go Back to Come Back

As I began the composition of this book, I didn't realize how much more freedom I would gain with each keystroke. The beginning was very hard because I had to go back to a very unfavorable place in life. Much of that place I would rather forget. But in understanding that everything happens for a reason, I realized that my past (no matter how indifferent I may feel about it) helped to develop my character. The rules and regulations were one thing, but the establishment and foundation introduced me to Jesus Christ as well as the power of the Almighty God. If not for that, I may not have had as much of an understanding. Some may argue that I am ignorant because I do not believe the same as they do. They are entitled to say so. But my comfort level is my concern.

Sometimes we have to go back to an unfavorable place to address a hurt we would rather forget for the duration of our life span. As hard as it may be, addressing that hurtful past helps to release a lot of suppressed anger as well as stress. We also do not go back in physical form but in spiritual form.

One professional explained that repetitiously telling someone we trust about a bad experience will help to release the hurt. The more the story is told, the easier it becomes to speak of it. Until the hurt becomes easier to talk about, maybe discussing it once daily or once a week would be feasible. I haven't tried this personally, but it makes sense due to my feeling relief after discussing difficult topics many times with loved ones. However, the method that best works for me with problem solving and expressing emotions is writing down those feelings and then destroying the evidence.

During one of my rare church visits in the past few years, I happened to finally visit one of my friend's churches for the first time. I had been previously invited to attend several times. During the sermon, the clergy member said to the congregation, "Go back and take what the devil has stolen from you and your family." The statement was made to the entire congregation, but I knew it was meant for me. Without him knowing my past or possibly not even realizing I was in attendance; he spoke these relevant words. Consider the writing of this book as the challenge being accepted.

As stated, during my infrequent visits to church, whether through praise or sermon, I always receive a special message from God. Most messengers do not know me personally or indirectly; but because they are in tune with one interconnecting harmonious spirit, they are able to speak relevant, discerning, and prophetic messages connected to the people within the congregation. Not every message is for everyone, so the message may not connect with certain individuals but does so with others.

How do we recognize when God is speaking to us? I'm sure there are those who can better explain; but from my experience, it is not a particular voice that can be described or a ghost-like experience. Sometimes the communication comes from another individual, a book, from within (God), a song, a prayer, a movie, a sign (such as nature or the weather), a movement, or any of many other avenues. More important is the feeling of satisfaction, assurance, or amazement that accompanies the communication.

Being superstitious is one thing but knowing when God is speaking is another. Usually, superstition comes with some type of followed pattern or ritual which, when followed, proves to be successful in producing or preventing certain results. If the pattern is not followed (such as not talking to a loved one before playing a game), an uneasy feeling resides, and paranoia settles. This deals with the psyche. If the pattern somehow ceases to produce the desired results, a new superstition may be ventured.

However, when God communicates with us, our faith plays a major factor. This comes with a calmer feeling of assurance regardless of circumstances or odds because God has spoken. No previous pattern or ritual is needed. God's word is true alone. There is a level of communication directly from God that allows one to be not only prewarned but also prepared for certain situations due to previous signs. The key difference in the two is the calm and certainty that come with God's communication. There are times when we may be uncertain about communication, but confirmation of reassurance always ensues.

Can we be superstitious and spiritual? Sure. We can be any way we choose. Both ways tend to work out fine for many. It is when we go overboard with superstition that we can create an issue such as unnecessary stress or spooky thinking. But to each his own.

We should never allow anyone to persuade us we do not have the privilege of God's communication. Some may have a better relationship because of the time taken to connect and establish it. Each person is responsible for doing so according to his or her preference. It's called free will.

CHAPTER 28:

Hidden Pieces of the Heart

F OR years I was unaware hatred and resentment lived in my heart. The hurt was deeply buried to the point it weighed down my mind, body, and spirit. It was not until I encountered a spiritual break through shared personally between me and God that I realized the magnitude of the weight.

That weight was causing physical as well as mental complications. Stress causes all kinds of unfavorable reactions to humans. From my experience, the more stress we are under, the less productively our brains operate. I was always an energetic person; but without realizing it, I became weighed down by an accumulation of things that absorbed that energy. Every problem seemed to pile on top of the others so that, little by little, the weight became heavier.

Realizing how much of my basic decision making was severely limited in childhood was upsetting. Aside from that, I certainly caused things to come upon myself because of poor decisions as an adult. It took some time to release some of the hurt and pain because I did not realize its source. Of course, resentment tried to settle in. The "what if" factor also came into play: What if we had been allowed to participate in academic sports as children? Would any of us have made it to professional leagues? What if we had been allowed to socialize more? Would we be more outgoing and fearless? The list goes on and on.

I once had animosity towards anyone who even invited me to church or mentioned the name of God. I had such bitterness in my heart that I couldn't stand to see certain individuals coming because I knew invitations to church would be one of the first things to come out of their mouths. I now do not mind the invitations because the decision to attend is according to my free will. I now have a spirituality that is dependent on God.

I questioned how God could allow certain things to happen to my family when my mother and father went to church plenty. When a loved one passed away, I questioned how God could take away someone I loved so much. I questioned how God could be so loving in one moment and seemingly so cruel the next. I questioned God a lot; but when I realized how much control God gives us as human beings that we choose not to exercise, I realized that we cause a lot of things to come upon ourselves.

Ultimately, although he is in control, we tend to try to put some of our responsibilities on God. Does God give us the ability to create our own realities? ☺ All in all, I personally believe that everything aligns according to God's plan. Some things cannot be explained because to us they make no sense such as, for example, an innocent baby passing away. There will always be inexplicable hurtful occurrences; but that doesn't mean because of the unfavorable end results we should give up on God or ourselves.

What also helped to release the hurt was realizing that things could always be worse and finding the positives that helped to relieve their grasp. The possibility of becoming a professional athlete didn't have to stop at the door of my parents' home. Once I moved out, I still had the opportunity to go to college and play sports if I chose to do so or even to try out for a team as a walk-on. But I decided against it.

I am still a sports fanatic, so sometimes, in the morning, I listen to sports radio. I love to watch NFL football (Go, Cowboys!) and NBA basketball. For me, it is a hobby that sometimes thrills and kills. One minute, I am thrilled because my team is winning; the next, figuratively speaking of course, I feel like strangling them because of their complete melt down or inexcusable loss. All in all, for me, the pros of watching sports far outweigh the cons.

Further, I am blessed that all my brothers and sisters are alive and well. We ate well and dressed well as children. Our parents were able to take good care of us and always taught us to stick together. Both were upright people of God and we could look to them as examples. We get along very well (most of the time), and we all love God. We are far from the perfect family, but what's life without a little crazy. ☺

I will forever be grateful for my roots. This book is not intended to upset anyone or to make them dislike me; but if that happens, so be it. The intent is to share my personal experiences with religion, brainwashing, and spirituality. It is my story. I hope, in some way shape, or form, it helps others.

CHAPTER 29:

Confronting the Hurt

M y challenge to those who have been hurt in any form of life—whether by family, friendship, religion, relationship, profession, or something similar—is to do as the clergy member suggested: Go back and take back what was taken.

If a relationship stole your heart, take it back. If someone took your self-esteem by violating you, take it back. If someone took your ability to say no, take it back. If someone took your voice, take it back. If someone or something took your confidence, take it back. If someone took your ability to trust, take it back. If someone caused you to misplace loyalty, find it. If someone wrongfully took materialistic things such as a car, a house, or money, take them back. (The court system can amicably handle this.) If someone took your opinion from you, take it back.

If someone took your ability to think for yourself, take it back. If your business closed due to financial hardship, take it back. If someone or something took your peace of mind, take it back. If someone took your dignity, take it back. If someone stole your respect, take it back. If someone took your smile, take it back. If someone took your happiness, take it back. If someone took your love, take it back. If someone took your truth, take it back. If someone took your understanding, take it back. If someone took your hope, take it back. If someone took your faith, take it back. If someone took your motivation in life, take it back. If someone took your clarity, take it back. If someone or something took your sobriety, take it back. Take it back, take it back, take it all-l-l back! ☺

The someone who takes these things from you does not have to be another person. It can be one of the many other "I" characters that hold many of our intangibles hostage. We alone rob ourselves of plenty. The effort to take things back is a process, but it is well worth the energy and time.

Unfortunately, some things, such as time or loved ones, we cannot take back because they have moved on to the next life. But those things we have control over, which are rightfully ours, we should take back.

The main reason I decided to write this book was because I, as well as others, have been hurt. I've personally experienced hurt that lasted for a very long time, with its origination points being elusive. The most hurtful part was realizing some of the origination points. The hurt was obvious to others, but I was oblivious as it penetrated my natural persona. It was buried deeply in my heart, which impacted my spirit. It showed in my demeanor, the words I spoke, and the way I treated others and myself.

This book is for all who have experienced a hurt that is so elusive it cannot be properly diagnosed even though its existence is certain. It's for those who understand the hurt and its source but are looking for a way to release the relentless internal pain. It's for those who feel the hurt holds them back from breaking into a new beginning.

The healing is inside of us; and inside, if we choose to look deeply enough, we will find God. Even if there is no belief in God, we should believe in self enough to look inside for healing. Circumstance sometimes says we can't because of heredity. Circumstance sometimes says we can't because of stacked odds. Circumstance says we dare not because it seems too complex. Sometimes the ones closest to us cause inexplicable pain that leaves us feeling vulnerable and alone. Even when we are alone, we have ourselves to push through. Accepting help from God makes it much easier.

So where is the hurt: Childhood? A relationship? A church? Home? A friend? Yourself? A place of business? An unknown place? God? I know eyebrows rose at the last question, but some acts upset us to the point we are upset with and hurt by God.

Whatever the source, when is it a good time to heal? Has it become so comfortable that changing is not a consideration? You are not changing for someone else but for self to fill the void with self-love, the void left by a loved one who walked out, the void left from a relationship that ended, the void left by abuse, the void left by broken promises, the void left by regret.

One of my toughest experiences was a confrontation with self, a confrontation with things such as bad habits that had negative impact. It was a confrontation that needed to go down! We are all flawed human beings, but we can surely make ourselves better. It is time to unlock the higher inner self we possess, our highest being that demonstrates a kind of supernatural power.

The past no longer has to control our present and surely not our future. It's okay to say I don't understand why, I feel loss, I'm confused.

It's okay to say and admit those things even as adults. Opening up expedites the healing process. It's okay to say we need help with this because we've tried and failed in the past. Where are you, God? Who are you, God? Can we get to know you, God? Help! We should tell our lower self that he or she can't have us because we are better and stronger.

Who cares what other people think if they are not there to help. They will not be there to see us through the hurt. They do not understand the internal pain. Acknowledgment of the pain is the first step in healing. If we need help, professionals are out there to assist us with breaking through barriers.

There is a better society that is not to be controlled by religious dictatorship but exists more in the freedom of self and God. Understanding self helps to better understand others and God. How can we not be powerful if we all come from God? This power can be accessed from the inside out.

One day fear will no longer be a tactic used to deter people from experiencing God for themselves. Ghost-like mentalities will disappear and be replaced with moments of clarity and freedom. Who said we can't? Why believe them? Why not believe we can? We choose what we believe or don't believe. Exercise the freedom that we have in the US of A.

Sure, there still and always will be things we have to confront because, again, we are human. Personally, I am far from perfect; nor do I try to be. There are certain acts we try to perfect, such as playing a tune, but that is different. I like being free to exercise the right to make mistakes and learn from them.

CHAPTER 30:

Freedom in Choosing to Be Happy

D o we have a choice? We have the hope of an afterlife that is so much better than this. Those leaders of churches who know they are holding people in captivity should let them go. Free them from low thinking and expectations. Help them thrive as individuals, not just survive. Better yet, if we know we are not free, we should set ourselves free. The words from "Go Down Moses," an old spiritual, come to mind: "Tell old pharaoh let my people go." It is one thing to be physically free; it is another to be mentally and spiritually free, which also connects with physicality. Unfortunately, many unanswered questions will remain a mystery until the afterlife.

The religious background, as well as the psychological transformation I went through, helped my development in becoming a more spiritual rather than a religious person. I do not particularly follow a set of religious rules or regulations but try to keep an open mind to change because time is rapidly doing so.

To me, the most important thing is happiness and peace of mind. If I never become a member of another church body, that will be fine with me. But the church definitely has a purpose, a purpose I will continually support; so it is great that so many are a part of our communities.

I believe happiness is most important to human beings. My happiness comes from loving myself, my family, and God. Those who choose to develop a personal relationship with God should start with daily acknowledgment, even if it is just a quick but meaningful thank you for another day.

We may need to make some modifications as we learn more of ourselves, of each other, and of God, should we choose. The world is constantly moving forward with innovations seemingly every second. They say there is nothing new under the sun, but some things are new to this life's cycle. I choose not to restrict myself to just one form of thinking. I'd much rather have a free mind and am working towards that each and every day of my life. I still struggle with some mental barriers and am in acceptance of that. But as I work, I am optimistic of one day conquering.

The best advice that I give to myself and try to follow is to be free in being myself and to be comfortable with decision making, even it seems a little peculiar to some, including me. I could not always exercise that right, so it feels good to be able to do so. By far, the content of this book focuses on intricate personal experiences and views concerning religion, brainwashing, and spirituality; however, this is just a small part of the many sides of me. I am a naturally shy person; but in certain situations, I rise to the occasion.

My spiritual rebirth has allowed me to understand how special I truly am as a person. I am grateful for another opportunity in life to fulfill what are now new dreams and visions that trump those previously envisioned.

My family and I are a special kind, dynamic and strong, even though some expectations were to keep us down and weak. I'm sure many will say I have lost my mind and am on my way to hell because I composed this book or believe in the way that I choose. But what's new? The only concern is my mental freedom and happiness that doesn't come at the expense of another's. That too should be of primary concern for others. But to each his own.

CONCLUSION

I TRULY hope reading this book has helped some to think outside of the box and into their own perspectives on the many possibilities that were once unseen. I understand the feeling of thinking in a box, which can be very difficult to escape. I am very grateful for those individuals who invented new thought processes concerning the more difficult topics, for without them, who knows?

Never in my wildest dreams did I think I would write a book sharing a certain part of myself. But this book is not about me. It is about a painted picture of the mind, body, spirit, and soul that needs to be modified and updated. There comes a time in life when certain things just don't matter to people, because the difficult times they have been through introduce them to new perspectives and appreciation for things once underappreciated.

Developing individual identity can be a very difficult task with so many influences to sway us one way or another. We sometimes lose ourselves in how other people would like to identify us. I am grateful for my life experiences thus far that have led me to conclude everything happens for a reason within a season.

Losing my mother was the most devastating occurrence in my life. I am hurt and I am angry. However, I am also grateful to God for the personal encounters shared with me before her passing. Otherwise, I may have completely lost faith. See, it is because of my personal experiences with God that I can better cope with the loss of my mother. Now I am left to trust God's plan and to allow time to heal the wounds.

Some of my family and I are into a new awakening; and I hope those who were gracious enough to take the time and diligence to read this book are also able to walk into their new awakening, whether it be spiritual, personal, emotional, physical, mental, psychological, or professional. God bless and be free. Let's go-o-o!

The end and on to a new beginning. ☺